T0360848

Power in Business Relationships

Focusing on the issue of power as the main building block of relationships between business buyers and sellers, this book explains the complex nature of power with its multidimensional and multi-directional character.

As a complex construct, inter-firm power is treated as a matter of perception as well as in terms of total and relative power. The book analyses extensively the issue of power asymmetry with its dynamics and its consequences for business-to-business (B2B) relationships, particularly analysing the dynamic mechanism of power. Various theoretical domains or research streams regarding managing an asymmetrical business relationship by the weaker partner are also examined. Based on the studies of other scholars as well as on the authors' own research, this book shows how weaker suppliers or buyers deal with high-power partners in business relationships and the approaches of more powerful parties to asymmetrical relationship development. Additionally, the book presents the specific nature of power in international B2B relationships, including its connection to culture and conflict, as well as how to handle power in managing export performance within international B2B relationships.

It is written for scholars and students who are interested in academic research concerning B2B marketing and B2B relationship marketing domains, specifically those who are interested in literature dealing with supply chain management, key account management, relationship portfolio management, distribution channel management and the network approach.

Dariusz Siemieniako is Associate Professor at Bialystok University of Technology and Kozminski University, both in Poland. His research focuses on interorganisational relationships versus social issues and also on B2B marketing, including power issues and collaborative innovation development. He has published in quality journals including: Industrial

Marketing Management, Journal of Business Research and Journal of Marketing Management. Dariusz serves as an associate editor or board member for several journals and, he is the founder and coordinator of the CID Group, an informal international network of researchers and journal editors. He was associated with Griffith University, Australia (2013–2019), most recently as Adjunct Associate Professor. He has seven years of business practice working as a CEO, Board Member and Director of Business Development for several companies operating in international environment on B2B markets.

Maciej Mitręga is a professor at the University of Economics in Katowice, where he serves as chair professor of the Discipline Board for Management Science and head of the Organizational Relationship Management Department. The majority of his work focuses on dynamic capabilities, but he also studies a wide range of topics in strategy and business-to-business areas. You can find his articles in periodicals such as the International Journal of Operations & Production Management, Long Range Planning Industrial Marketing Management, Journal of Business Research and International Marketing Review. In some of these journals Maciej serves as guest editor or board member. In 2010–2011, Maciej worked at Manchester Business School as a Marie Curie Research Fellow.

Hannu Makkonen is Professor of Marketing at the School of Marketing and Communication at the University of Vaasa. His research interests lie in the areas of innovation management, innovation ecosystems, and value creation logics in industrial networks and relationships. His previous work has been published in e.g. Industrial Marketing Management, Technovation, Journal of Business Research, Marketing Theory, Journal of Service Management, Journal of Business & Industrial Marketing, Management Decision, Technology Analysis & Strategic Management, Journal of Business Market Management and Journal of Financial Services Marketing.

Gregor Pfajfar is an associate professor in the field of international business at School of Economics and Business, University of Ljubljana. His main area of research focuses on distribution channel conflicts and relationships in B2B markets, international marketing strategies, export performance and collaborative consumption. As a visiting professor he gave lectures at internationally high-ranked universities in England, Canada, Russia, Poland, Lithuania, Estonia and Croatia. He was a project leader or a team member for several applied projects in the field of international business for selected international companies like P&G, IBM, BMW, Henkel, Gorenje, Elan, etc. His work was published in Industrial Marketing Management, International Marketing Review, Journal of Services Marketing, Journal of Business and Industrial marketing, European Journal of International Management, Journal of East European Management Studies among others.

Routledge Focus on Business and Management

The fields of business and management have grown exponentially as areas of research and education. This growth presents challenges for readers trying to keep up with the latest important insights. *Routledge Focus on Business and Management* presents small books on big topics and how they intersect with the world of business.

Individually, each title in the series provides coverage of a key academic topic, whilst collectively, the series forms a comprehensive collection across the business disciplines.

Pop-Up Retail
The Evolution, Application and Future of Ephemeral Stores
Ghalia Boustani

Building Virtual Teams
Trust, Culture, and Remote Work
Catalina Dumitru

Fostering Wisdom at Work
Jeff M. Allen

Artificial Intelligence, Business and Civilization
Our Fate Made in Machines
Andreas Kaplan

Power in Business Relationships
Dynamics, Strategies and Internationalisation
*Dariusz Siemieniako, Maciej Mitręga, Hannu Makkonen
and Gregor Pfajfar*

For more information about this series, please visit: www.routledge.com/
Routledge-Focus-on-Business-and-Management/book-series/FBM

Power in Business Relationships

Dynamics, Strategies and Internationalisation

Dariusz Siemieniako, Maciej Mitręga, Hannu Makkonen and Gregor Pfajfar

The book has been reviewed by Assoc. Prof. Milena Ratajczak-Mrozek and Assoc. Prof. Marek Zieliński.

Routledge
Taylor & Francis Group
LONDON AND NEW YORK

First published 2023
by Routledge
4 Park Square, Milton Park, Abingdon, Oxon OX14 4RN

and by Routledge
605 Third Avenue, New York, NY 10158

Routledge is an imprint of the Taylor & Francis Group, an informa business

© 2023 Dariusz Siemieniako, Maciej Mitręga, Hannu Makkonen and Gregor Pfajfar

The right of Dariusz Siemieniako, Maciej Mitręga, Hannu Makkonen and Gregor Pfajfar to be identified as authors of this work has been asserted in accordance with sections 77 and 78 of the Copyright, Designs and Patents Act 1988.

Trademark notice: Product or corporate names may be trademarks or registered trademarks, and are used only for identification and explanation without intent to infringe.

British Library Cataloguing-in-Publication Data
A catalogue record for this book is available from the British Library

Library of Congress Cataloging-in-Publication Data
A catalog record for this book has been requested

ISBN: 978-0-367-54992-3 (hbk)
ISBN: 978-0-367-55979-3 (pbk)
ISBN: 978-1-003-09593-4 (ebk)

DOI: 10.4324/9781003095934

Typeset in Times New Roman
by Apex CoVantage, LLC

Contents

Acknowledgements

The part of the research conducted by Maciej Mitręga was supported by National Science Centre Poland (PL – 'Narodowe Centrum Nauki'): [Grant Number UMO2017/25/B/HS4/01669].

Introduction

The concept of power occupies a central position in various academic literature. From the perspective of business-to-business marketing and interorganisational relationships, an extensive body of research exists (e.g. Shamsollahi et al., 2020). This research has explicated how power shapes actor-to-actor interaction, the development of the mutual relationship and relationship outcomes (Cowan et al., 2015; Cox, 2001). The research has provided tools and perspectives that imply practical relevance for managers in analysing different types of opportunities and threats with the company either being a potential power source or a power target. However, in modern business practice where companies are part of far-reaching business networks, the manifestations of power are also versatile. Connected through multiple direct and indirect collaborative and competitive relationships, the bases of power are subject to constant change and rely on actors' capacity to perceive their own position with regard to that of other parties. On the broadest level, inter-organisational relationships and supply chains feature supranational competition and global politics demonstrated by, for instance, competition between Asian, European and Northern American companies and their networks. These multi-level contexts of business relationships and networks challenge previous studies on power based on individual relationships and the idea of inter-individual dependence. At the same time, the complex setup of the modern business landscape, and the inherent character of the power concept as partly a sum of the features of the power source as well as the perceptions of these by the power target, makes the study of power in business relationships a timely topic with tremendous opportunities for practical implication and academic contributions. This book aims to build towards a systemic perspective (see Meehan & Wright, 2012) and dynamic presentation (Lacoste & Johnsen, 2015; Pérez & Cambra-Fierro, 2015) of power in order to facilitate both managers and academic researchers in their endeavours to explicate the multifaceted concept of power and its practical implications.

DOI: 10.4324/9781003095934-1

The first chapter focuses on power-related tactics in asymmetrical buyer-supplier relationships. It explicates 1) the motivations to undertake power-related tactics by the weaker side of the relationship, 2) the actions the weaker supplier in the relationship may take with respect to improving its power position in order to increase value from the relationship with stronger buyers, 3) the division of these tactics into intentional and non-intentional activities, 4) the positive or negative effect of power asymmetry/ symmetry on the consequences of the relationship and the performance of the actors. On this basis, the chapter explores a multidimensional power asymmetry continuum that facilitates identification of the status of all mediated and non-mediated power sources between the actors to the relationship. Similarly, the chapter provides a discussion on resources and power in working relationships between organisations, and presents a power-benefit matrix for these issues. The conclusion of Chapter 1 is that power position improvement should be treated as a long-lasting management process aimed at getting closer to a "relationship golden mean" within the constraints of the wider relational structures that surround a business dyad. This means that attempts aiming to make full use of power asymmetry could be economically ineffective, and that instead, attention should be paid to finding an appropriate level of interdependence between the buyer and seller.

The second chapter provides an overview of relationship power dynamics in scientific research. Particularly, the chapter discusses the concept of power, synthesises a power dynamics canvas and introduces a narrative approach discussing the opportunities for its use in the study of power dynamics in business relationships. The power dynamics canvas and the narrative techniques reviewed in the chapter provide a basis for gathering a thick set of micro-narratives and for building towards macro narratives that may be used for defining a community of practice and for development of theory. The theoretical perspectives are condensed from the informants' and researchers' narratives and produced through balanced use of the power dynamics canvas and narrative techniques. These are likely to yield a rich, multi-level theoretical account of power dynamics, which will provide guidance both for managers in dealing with power issues, as well as for researchers in advancing the scientific field.

The third chapter explores power in international business relationships. In particular, the discussion revolves around culture and conflict as antecedents to power, and export performance as a power outcome in international business relationships. The chapter concludes that cultural and power distance are critical for international business relationships, particularly for headquarters-subsidiary relationships and conflict resolution strategies. Furthermore, the chapter shows that coercive power negatively influences functional conflict and positively affects dysfunctional conflict, while non-coercive power positively influences functional conflict and negatively affects dysfunctional conflict. Strategies for conflict resolution are identified and discussed in terms of the assertiveness and cooperativeness of international business partners as linked to the exercising of the types of power available.

The three chapters described above provide authentic, stand-alone contributions. However, together they build towards a systemic approach to shed light on and explicate the various elements of power and power dynamics in order to develop the theory and practice of power in business relationships. The book is based on academic research, but the writing style and the various frameworks and classifications we present are also designed to appeal to the casual (non-scientific) reader interested in increasing their understanding of power dynamics.

References

Cowan, K., Paswan, A. K., & Van Steenburg, E. (2015). When inter-firm relationship benefits mitigate power asymmetry. *Industrial Marketing Management*, 48, 140–148.

Cox, A., Watson, G., Lonsdale, C., & Sanderson, J. (2004). Managing appropriately in power regimes: Relationship and performance management in 12 supply chain cases. *Supply Chain Management: International Journal*, 9(5), 357–371.

Lacoste, S., & Johnsen, E. (2015). Supplier–customer relationships: A case study of power dynamics. *Journal of Purchasing and Supply Management*, 21, 229–240.

Meehan, J., & Wright, G. H. (2011). Power priorities: A buyer–seller comparison of areas of influence. *Journal of Purchasing and Supply Management*, 17(1), 32–41.

Pérez, L., & Cambra-Fierro, J. (2015). Learning to work in asymmetric relationships: Insights from the computer software industry. *Supply Chain Management: An International Journal*, 20(1), 1–10.

Shamsollahi, A., Chmielewski-Raimondo, D. A., Bell, S. J., & Kachouie, R. (2020). Buyer–supplier relationship dynamics: A systematic review. *Journal of the Academy of Marketing Science*, 1–19.

1 Power as the cornerstone of business relationships

1.1 Multifaceted power as a key building block of business relationships

1.1.1 Introduction

The power concept has played a central role in the development of marketing thought from early research on power in marketing channels (Gaski, 1984, 1986; Lusch, 1976; Siemieniako et al., 2021) and purchasing (Bonoma, 1982; Kraljic, 1987) to a more recent approach picturing power as a general phenomenon in inter-organisational relationships (see Meehan & Wright, 2012; Cowan et al., 2015; Johnsen et al., 2020). However, the literature on power in inter-organisational structures is deeply rooted in theories about power in society in general, which would seem to be highly appropriate as inter-organisational relations are embedded within wider social structures, and the demarcation between these two is always problematic (Czernek-Marszałek, 2020; Hagedoorn & Frankort, 2008; Ratajczak-Mrozek, 2017). In this chapter, we briefly present the meaning of power and its evolution in business-to-business literature, while at the same time we show how this meaning relates to the wider discourse in the social sciences.

1.1.2 Power and power sources in business relationships

The literature recognised early on that power goes beyond physically enforcing the actions of one person over another, and recognised the multifaceted nature of power in social relations. French and Raven (1959) proposed analysing power using several different types of power, that is reward, coercive, legitimate, referent and expert, while each of these "power sources" represent the potential for influencing the other actor. In 1965, this categorisation was enriched by a sixth source of power, namely informational power (Raven, 1965). French and Raven (1959) perceived power as a change in

DOI: 10.4324/9781003095934-2

an actor's behaviour or beliefs that result from the actions of another actor (French & Raven, 1959; Raven, 1965). The initial proposal by French and Raven (1959) has been revisited, and as a result certain specific variations of power bases have been proposed, such as personal and impersonal forms of coercion and reward, positive and negative forms of expertise and reference, as well as contract-based or norms-based legitimate power (Raven, 1992). Numerous further studies on inter-organisational relations using French and Raven (1959) categorised power sources into two groups; coercive and other power sources, in which expert, referent, legitimate and reward power were classified as non-coercive (e.g. Cowan et al., 2015; Frazier & Summers, 1984; Handley & Benton, 2012; Wilkinson, 1973; Wilkinson, 1996; Siemieniako & Mitręga, 2019). In a similar spirit, power sources were also divided into mediated and non-mediated power (Nyaga et al., 2013; Benton & Maloni, 2005; Siemieniako & Mitręga, 2019). In this second typology, the mediated power sources, that is legitimate, coercive and reward, are sometimes treated as negative forces that restrict the development of relationships (Benton & Maloni, 2005; Siemieniako & Mitręga, 2019). The distinct concepts of power based on French and Raven's (1959) proposal and further developments are presented in brief in Table 1.1.

1.1.3 Power as socially constructed phenomenon

The social sciences tend to see power in social relations as more and more strongly connected with the concepts of truth and knowledge, especially in the works of cultural theorists and constructivists. Even in the earliest works on power in society, the relativistic meaning of power was somehow visible, i.e. that power is not an objective phenomenon but rather a subjective one. For example, according to Emerson (1962), whose power-dependence conceptualisation became one of most inspirational theories in literature on power, "power is a property of the social relation; it is not an attribute of the actor" (p. 32). Consequently, Emerson (1962) defined the power of one actor over another in the perceived dependence on the realisation of certain goals based on the other actors' actions vis-à-vis the possibility to realise these goals outside the relationship. Foucault (1977), who was interested mostly in power exhibited in large social structures, suggested that "power is everywhere" as it is embodied in public discourse, so it is not necessarily something that can be attributed to a given person or even group of people, but instead is seen as dispersed within social structures. In this approach, the terms power and truth might be used interchangeably as they both refer to what is acceptable within society at a given point in time. Therefore, power dynamics may be perceived as a struggle between different ways of deciding what is true and false, which can be observed in the media and between various ideologies.

Table 1.1 Brief definitions of principal power sources discussed in the literature

Type of power sources	Definition
Mediated power sources	
Coercive	Coercive power is the potential of one firm to employ punishment to influence another firm's behaviour. Molm (1997) and Yeung et al. (2009) provided examples of using coercive power sources such as: imposing financial penalties, withholding important support or reward or threatening to withdraw from an initial promise (Siemieniako & Mitręga, 2019).
	Personal coercion takes the form of a threat of rejection of one actor by another or the imposition of penalties, while impersonal coercion refers to the belief that another actor has the real possibility to psychically threaten or impose penalties on the actor.
Legitimate	Legitimate power refers to the ability of one actor to impose feelings of obligation to act or think in certain way on another actor. As such, legitimate power reflects in some ways formal or informal authority. Legitimate power may be based on a contract written and signed by the parties, but it can also be based on cultural values, e.g. the social norm of reciprocity or the norm of social responsibility, that is helping someone who requires assistance (French, 1959).
Reward	Reward power relates to using rewards to affect another actor's behaviour. The reward might be either impersonal, in which case it takes the form of promising to make certain valuable resources available to the actor based on conditions, e.g. money or social recognition. However, it can be also personal, when the promised reward reflects the promise of approving the initiation of a relationship with the other actor. In the latter case, being engaged in the desired relationship is the reward itself (Raven, 1992).
Non-mediated power sources	
Expert	When one party in the relationship has expert power, this means that they possess expertise and knowledge that the other party wants (Palmatier et al., 2006). The expert power may take on a positive form if the actor believes that the other actor's knowledge is correct, which is why the actor follows the expert's instructions. However, it can also be negative if the actor acts against the expert's instructions due to a feeling that the expert is driven only by personal gain (Raven, 1992).
Referent	According to Nyaga et al. (2013, p. 47), referent power exists when one firm admires the way another conducts its operations and therefore values being identified with it (Siemieniako & Mitręga, 2019). This form of power is related to the need to be affiliated with groups of organisations that we value and aspire to.

Type of power sources	Definition
Informational	This form of power is based on the unequal distribution of valuable information between actors. Knowing that some information would be much appreciated by the other actor, an actor may gradually provide only partial information on the condition the other side acts in a certain way (Raven, 1965). In the business context, informational power may be perceived as a specific variation of expert power because, as Maloni and Benton (2000, p. 9) argued, *"expert power refers to the perception that one firm holds information or expertise (such as product or process leadership) that is valued by another firm"* (Siemieniako & Mitręga, 2019).

It is also based on the assumption that every physical or non-physical object has no fixed meaning, and instead its understanding emerges through the language and the social practices connected to these objects, i.e. power is an inherent characteristic of discourse, and determines how we talk about something and what we do about what we say. Consequently, resistance to power takes the form of recognising and questioning norms that are commonly accepted, for example, in terms of questioning what people think is good vs bad or productive vs non-productive. In a similar spirit, Gramsci (1971), who is known especially for his work on cultural hegemony, proposed that power is enacted through the media imposing meaning for things within the discourse, while, in turn, the media are restrained by ruling organisation and social groups. The effect is that power takes the form of building common sense with regard to how we see things and how we act upon things. This process crosses the boundaries of a given national economy, and may be seen as a mechanism for building global hegemony. Bourdieu (1979) proposed the concept of symbolic power, which refers to various processes through which existing social habits and hierarchies are maintained between the dominators and the dominated. Bourdieu (1979) suggested that cultural capital is actually even more important than economic capital in establishing hierarchies in societies. In this approach, attempts to change one's position within society are very much connected with changing one's own and others' cognition. One may act by trying to transform the categories of perception and appreciation of the social world, and the cognitive and evaluative structures through which it is constructed (Bourdieu, 1989, p. 20).

Notably, Foucault is one of the few philosophers who recognises that power can be a necessary, productive and positive force in society, rather than just a repressive force that forces us to do things we do not want to do (Gaventa, 2001). In this view, power is the cornerstone of society as it produces ways for people to coexist and exchange views, and organises the actions of multiple actors. The existence of power leads to norms in society that discipline people's behaviour without wilful use of power in a coercive way. Such an approach is gaining more and more followers in business-to-business research, where power inequalities are inherent and are a legitimate feature of business relationships (Blois, 2010; Håkansson, 1982; Wilkinson & Kipnis, 1978). The literature provides some empirical evidence that using coercive power can actually lead to win-win situations in business relationships. Yeung et al. (2009) found that using coercive power helps in achieving better supply chain integration. Vos et al. (2021) provided evidence that using coercion does not lead to a decrease in a partner's satisfaction in B2B relationships if the partner perceives the status of the focal company as appropriate. In a similar vein, Jain et al. (2014) found that relationship commitment mitigates the negative link between using coercion and trust in B2B relationships. A study by Pulles et al. (2014) suggests that using coercive power does not decrease a partner's inclination to engage in cooperative investments in buyer-seller relationships. Moreover, when a relationship is based on a large share of the turnover of the focal company, the use of coercive power by the partner may even increase the inclination of the focal company to contribute to the relationship with additional physical investments. In the specific context of Web-enabled supply chains, Mora-Monge et al. (2019) noticed that using coercive power did not decrease the partner's inclination to integrate with the supply chain. However, it should be emphasised that while non-coercive power is almost always portrayed as something positive, there is a stream of research that treats coercive power as a negative or dysfunctional aspect of buyer-seller relationships (Benton & Maloni, 2005). Generally, some researchers argue that exchange partners should avoid using coercive power (Leonidou et al., 2017; Benton & Maloni, 2005; Zadykowicz et al., 2020), as the use of coercive power results in negative effects such as distance, opportunism and uncertainty in the relationship, which in turn leverage infidelity in buyer-seller relationships, e.g. searching for alternative partners or initiating new business relations (Leonidou et al., 2017). Using coercive power was also found to be associated with problematic supply chain integration, either directly or indirectly (Fu et al., 2020; Huo et al., 2019; Zhang et al., 2020). Interestingly, as there is mixed evidence for the effects that using coercive power brings to business relationships, Horak and Long (2018) proposed that this issue can be solved by looking at the power phenomenon from the perspective of cultural differences. Specifically, Horak and Long (2018) suggested that the concept of Yin-Yang embedded in Taoist ideas provides an explanation as to why some Asian organisations accept a balance between power and trust in their collaborative business relationships. This complementary perspective on the influence of coercive vs non-coercive power was illustrated by supply chain relations in the automotive industry, and the authors (Ibid.) proposed some specific networking tactics for harmonising both of these aspects in effective business relationships, i.e. authority, delegation, community spirit, paternalistic benevolence, collaboration and commitment.

Business to business literature has made only partial use of the developments of power concepts in the social sciences, and power measures are usually premature (Hopkinson & Blois, 2014), however, the literature reflects increasing interest in the power concept, including its multifaceted nature and power dynamics (e.g. Makkonen et al., 2021). In general, as the context of focus widens from the inter-individual context to the inter-organisational context, the issue of power becomes ever more multi-dimensional and intertwined with the various temporal (past-present-future) and hierarchical (individual, organisation, relationship) dimensions that are inherent features of business relationships (see e.g. Makkonen & Olkkonen, 2017). This multiplicity produces a variety of viewpoints on power, some rigid and operating on one dimension, for example focusing on individuals (Wilson, 2000) or organisations (e.g. Sanderson, 2004) as the sources of power, while others are more inclusive and synthesise the individual, organisational and relationship levels into overarching accounts of power (see Meehan & Wright, 2012). Not all authors follow the power concept nomenclature proposed by French and Raven (1959). For example, Manaresi and Uncles (1995) use the "soft" versus "hard" power dichotomy, Johnson et al. (1993) use the notions of aggressive (i.e. legitimate and referent) and non-aggressive power (i.e. other forms), while Fu et al. (2020) categorise power among supply chain partners into economic (i.e. mediating rewards or punishment awarded to the other party) and non-economic power (other power sources). Here we align with Hopkinson and Blois (2014), who claim that these terms are frequently juxtaposed, which produces confusion in the whole research area. As other typologies proposed in the literature seem to reflect the main characteristics of the original typology, we are of the opinion that the conceptualisation by French and Raven (1959) and its further developments, i.e. coercive vs non-coercive, and mediated vs non-mediated power, are well supported in empirical studies and still have the potential to advance our understanding of power in business relationships.

1.1.4   *Structural and behavioural power asymmetry*

Power in business relationships can be analysed from two angles: the power structure, i.e. the asymmetry of power at a given point in time, or in the dynamic sense (1) and power behaviour, i.e. the instances of relationship partners using power (2) (Oukes et al., 2019). When it comes to

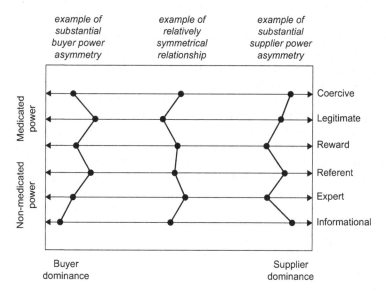

Figure 1.1 Multidimensional power asymmetry in buyer-seller relationships
Source: Siemieniako and Mitręga (2019)

structural power, the buyer-seller dyad can be perceived in terms of multi-faceted asymmetry, i.e. with the amalgamation of different power sources. To illustrate this, we present how power asymmetry can be visualised in a simulated business relationship (Figure 1.1.). The existence of power in a dyadic buyer-supplier relationship hints at one party being more powerful and thus the relationship being asymmetrical in power (Cox et al., 2007). The substantial asymmetry has been linked to both negative and positive consequences in the literature. The negative side underlines the harmful effects of power asymmetry in B2B relationships such as the high-power party neglecting the low-power party (Wolfe & McGinn, 2005; Siemieniako & Mitręga, 2019), the limited effectiveness of cooperative initiatives (Pfeffer & Salanick, 1978; Ulrich & Barney, 1984; Siemieniako & Mitręga, 2019), conflicts and a repressive atmosphere (Ojansivu et al., 2013), and low stability and poor relationship outcomes (see Hingley et al., 2015; Rokkan & Haughland, 2002). However, as with the general phenomenon of coercive power, positively-oriented works consider power asymmetry as a stabilising force that clarifies the role structure and decision-making in the relationship (see Hingley, 2005; Caniëls & Gelderman, 2007; Clemens & Douglas, 2006).

Power use, or so-called behavioural power (Oukes et al., 2019) is a very important aspect of power research because it refers to actions taken by relationship partners either to benefit from the existing power structure or to change the existing power structure (Lacoste & Johnsen, 2015; Siemieniako & Mitręga, 2018a; Siemieniako & Kaliszewski, 2022). This aspect can also be analysed with regard to variation of power sources, and in such case reflects actions dedicated to specific power bases, e.g. threats about coercive power and promises of reward power. In line with this, Frazier and Summers (1984) earlier described influence techniques as coercive (threats, legal pleas and promises) and non-coercive (recommendations, requests and information exchange). Generally, coercive influence refers to action modes which put "direct pressure on the target to perform a specific behavior or set of behaviors, with adverse consequences of noncompliance stressed and mediated by the source" (Gassenheimer & Ramsey, 1994). Meanwhile, non-coercive influence strategies are "those primarily centering on the beliefs and attitudes of the target about general business issues and involving little, if any, direct pressure from the source" (Frazier & Rody, 1991, pp. 53–54; Mishra & Banerjee, 2019). This distinction was to a large extent maintained in later research on power influence tactics (e.g. Boyle et al., 1992; Chang & Huang, 2012; Geyskens et al., 1999; Lai, 2007). Correspondingly, Mishra and Banerjee (2019) recently proposed the concept of non-coercive influence behaviour measured on a 12-item scale. Non-coercive influence is a construct composed of three dimensions: collaborative intent (i.e. the inclination to collaborate for mutual benefit), market intelligence dissemination (i.e. sharing valuable market knowledge with partners), and operational support (i.e. providing voluntary operational support to partners). It was also found to be connected with a partner's intention to engage in collaborative behaviour (Mishra and Banerjee, 2019), so indeed it could be concluded that such an approach is effective in influencing partners by changing their beliefs. However, the study by Mishra and Banerjee (2019) was conducted in the context of retail-centric supply chain management (R-SCM) (Randall et al., 2011), which means that such non-coercive influence strategies may only be useful in the case of dominating companies, whereas organisations that are dominated, and consequently are not as resourceful, might have to use other techniques. Other researchers focused explicitly on tactics used by small organisations, specifically suppliers in their relationships with dominating market players. Here, they identified non-coercive strategies related to extending technological and market competencies, as well as partner-specific investments (Lacoste & Johnsen, 2015; Pérez & Cambra-Fierro, 2015; Siemieniako & Mitręga, 2018; Siemieniako & Kaliszewski, 2022). Notably, the non-coercive influence concept correlates well with the works of social constructivists (Foucault, 1977; Bourdieu, 1979, 1989), who theorise that power is a process through which certain groups of people and organisations retain control over how other people think and feel. Specifically, all the non-coercive influence tactics used by the focal company comprise various methods for changing the way the focal company is perceived by their cooperating companies, either in upstream or downstream working relationships. The main difference between the non-coercive tactics used by dominated and dominating organisations relates to the direction in which the focal company wishes their partners to modify their thinking. Specifically, dominating companies are usually perceived as highly resourceful in both financial and non-financial terms (e.g. strong brand). However, they usually demand substantial non-retrievable adaptations from their partners, so their influencing tactics are oriented towards creating the perception of potentially long-term win-win cooperation. In this way they can reduce potential concerns from the smaller actor related to the risk of unfair distribution of the relationship pie (Dyer & Singh, 1998; Dyer et al., 2008). In contrast, dominated organisations (e.g. small suppliers) are usually only in the process of building their market position, and as such cannot switch counterparts so easily as big players can, so their non-coercive tactics are mainly oriented at building an image of a highly motivated partner equipped with unique resources and capabilities. Therefore, in research on supply chains, distribution channels and applying the constructivist perspective, behavioural non-coercive power in asymmetrical business relationships might be perceived as a communication process, more specifically market signalling, i.e. a means of communication that serves to provide more information in addition to just the literal message - "a message within a message" (Herbig, 1996, p. 35).

The causal connection between the behavioural and structural aspects of power (Oukes et al., 2019) could be presented as the relationship between resources, power position (structural power) and power tactics (behavioural power). Such a picture employs assumptions from resource-based theory (Pfefer & Salancik, 1978; Pfeffer, 1987), in which economic actors influence each other through unequal access to resources, which in turn creates dependencies between them. The rarer and more concentrated the valuable resource they possess is, the more dependence exists, however, mutual dependence translates into a certain form of mutual influence. These relations between two hypothetical organisations (A and B) are presented in Figure 1.2. However, apart from providing actual access to valuable resources, business partners (i.e. the buying company or selling company) can use various tactics to signal access to resources to the other side in an amount that is exaggerated or even fake. Additionally, the relationship between resources and power is not unidirectional. Instead, business relationships are usually asymmetrical, which leads to an unequal share of

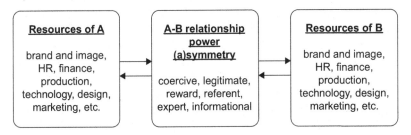

Figure 1.2 Resources and power in the working relationship between organisations A and B

relational benefits (Dyer & Singh, 1998; Dyer et al., 2008). Therefore, it is not only that resource differences between partners determine power asymmetry, but also that such asymmetries and instances of power use lead to a revised resource structure in the working relationship. In long-term relationships, such a reciprocal mechanism may either lead to maintaining initial resource-power disproportions, or to balancing multi-faced power and the resource structure between business partners (Pérez & Cambra-Fierro, 2015; Siemieniako & Mitręga, 2018a; Siemieniako & Kaliszewski, 2022). Importantly, a more balanced structure such as this does not necessarily mean that business partners achieve similar access to similar resources/ similar power forms, but that the structure becomes more balanced in that it becomes similarly difficult for both partners to switch to another partner.

Although power asymmetry and power use, including non-coercive and coercive influence, were accepted by some researchers quite early on as a legitimate element of business-to-business relationships (Blois, 2010; Håkansson, 1982; Wilkinson & Kipnis, 1978), research on power use is far from reaching a consensus. We have already presented many empirical studies that illustrate the outcome differences of using power in a coercive vs a non-coercive way. An interesting perspective comes from differentiating between power use and power abuse (Low & Li, 2019). To successfully use power, one must attempt to better the lives of both parties, or attempt to better the life of just one party without injuring the other. When there is an abuse of power, only one party's life is made better at the expense of the other (Low & Li, 2019). However, in business practice, the distinction is rarely clear, i.e. not bipolar, as there are many financial and non-financial benefits that can be implicit as a consequence of power use. For example, it is quite common practice for international retail chains to impose strict pricing conditions and additional "extra costs" on their suppliers without really thinking about their financial well-being (Mishra & Banerjee, 2019; Randall et al., 2011). This sometimes causes suppliers to drop out of the market, especially in crisis periods when there is tendency to externalise financial problems on "other" partners in the supply chain (Mitręga & Choi, 2021). However, it is not clear if this is simply one side ripping off the other, especially if we consider the learning benefits and guarantee of high contracted turnover that might be enjoyed by the supplier either in a short-term or long-term perspective (Siemieniako & Mitręga, 2018a). It is therefore appropriate to analyse power in buyer-seller relationships from the perspective of interaction between power and expected benefits, as proposed by Cowan et al. (2015). According to this, in asymmetrical B2B relationships, the general power structure and even every instance of power use in a B2B relationship can be analysed using the matrix presented in Figure 1.3.

The concept of hegemony brings an interesting angle to understanding what sometimes happens in asymmetrical inter-firm relationships. Similarly to the constructivist view on power, Johnsen et al. (2020) emphasised the cultural aspect of power in business relationships. Specifically, apart from the coercive dominance of the powerful party over the weaker one, e.g. through the use of one-sided contracts or by requesting extra dedicated effort, the stronger organisation controls the behaviour of weaker organisations through the ideology that is commonly accepted through the supply chain. Such ideology manifests itself in focal organisation superiority in terms of its exceptional image and widely appreciated knowledge and experience. In turn, such superiority translates into a hegemonic ability to maintain the status quo and existing ideologies. According to Johnsen et al. (2020), the concept of hegemony goes beyond the concept of power in interorganisational relationships as it reaches further than contractual and market dominance to encompass influence over commonly accepted values in society. Similarly to the constructivists' view on power (Foucault, 1977; Bourdieu, 1979), the concept of hegemony in asymmetric customer-supplier relationships assumes that while dominating organisations can implement conscious strategies of agential domination, the ideology that is maintained by such strategies is usually unconsciously accepted by average market

	Benefits below expected	Benefits at or above expected
High coercive power use	EXPLOITATIVE RELATIONSHIP	TOLERABLE RELATIONSHIP
Low coercive power use	AWKWARD RELATIONSHIP	IDEAL RELATIONSHIP

Figure 1.3 Power-benefit matrix in B2B relationships (perspective of the dominated partner)

Source: Adapted from Cowan et al. (2015)

players. Johnsen et al. (2020, p. 73) emphasise that in contrast to the influence based purely on power, hegemonic dominance is based on ideological influence achieved through voluntary consent. Therefore, there are various possible situations in the context of hegemonic inter-firm relationships; hegemonic organisations may be more or less active in pursuing ideological control, while weaker organisations may either conform with the status quo or engage in re-balancing or resistance strategies. Although Johnsen et al. (2020) explicitly positioned the concept of hegemony only in the context of asymmetric customer-supplier relationships, particularly in international supply chains where transnationals orchestrate large numbers of suppliers, the concept seems to be relevant to all asymmetric inter-firm relationships, including both upstream and downstream relationships as well as local business networks. Although hegemonic relationships are perceived as common in contemporary markets as they stabilise them around some commonly accepted rules of behaviour, they also have a negative function in the wider sense as they are linked to unstable and abusive labour practices. They also result in smaller enterprises being oriented toward shorter-term decisions, instead of providing them with space for more ambitious strategies and improving their positions within international value chains.

Overall, the review of B2B literature (i.e. supply chain and channel management) suggests that power is a very complex phenomenon that encompasses several dimensions/forms that may be grouped into two main categories: coercive and non-coercive. There is also a difference between power and power use, but a full understanding of power in inter-firm relationships requires employing the constructivists' approach to power, i.e. incorporating its cultural/perceptual meaning. There is a need to employ the relativistic nature of the concept of power: inter-firm power is about the objective properties of the powerful party, as well as the other party's perception of the influence (see Blois & Lacoste, 2009; Kähkönen & Lintukangas, 2011). This is especially true when it comes to the measurement of power in business-to-business relationships, which does not equal identification of objective differences in resource magnitude between business partners, especially different company size (Hopkinson & Blois, 2014). However, one should also take into consideration that not all power and power use is acknowledged by dominated actors, as ideological influences are usually based on spatial consensus and values dispersed among a large number of business actors. This, in turn, is linked to the need to sometimes look beyond the dyadic perspective, i.e. the relationship between a dominating customer/supplier and a dominated supplier/customer. Power can also be analysed in terms of the wider circumstances and indirect effects through which actor A has power over actor B via actor C. In this regard, in the multi-dimensional context of business relationships

(Makkonen & Olkkonen, 2017), the perception and use of power can be based on elements that bind a dyadic relationship to a network of other actors, and can dictate the degree of dependence of the dyadic actors as well as the power present in the relationship.

An interesting angle from which to analyse power is the cultural perspective, but not only in terms of the cultural or ideological influence of strong global organisations over smaller players, but also in terms of differences in national cultures with regard to power. In fact, claims that the acceptance of using different power tactics in business relationships may be culturally dependent appeared quite early in the literature, especially in international business research. For example, Johnson et al. (1993) found that in distribution channels, Western partners treat legitimate and referent power as non-aggressive power forms, while Japanese partners perceive them as rather aggressive. These results might not however be universal for all Asian countries. Lee (2001) provided evidence that Chinese distributors react negativelly to only coercive power use by other distribution channel members, while referent, expert, information, legitimate and reward power are treated as non-coercive, non-aggressive manifestations of power. According to Scheer et al. (2003), perceptions of injustice in the United States and the Netherlands are more tied to culturally influenced methods for measuring equity. Horak and Long (2018) proposed a harmonised use of coercive and non-coercive influence in supply chains composed of several tactics, but they suppose that some of these tactics may be very difficult to implement, e.g. paternalistic benevolence, as they can build very negative associations with regard to some social policies and values in the West. Looking at the equality movements dominating public discourse in Western countries, implementing "authority" tactics may also be problematic as it would assume that similar attention is paid to the value of competence and relationships alike across all supply chain connections. In general,

> there are differences in cultural understandings of power relations, different effects in the use of power and difficulties in applying western systems of measurement. Power-base theory, as applied to western channels, may neglect and/or give inappropriate emphasis to aspects of power that are most salient to the operation of marketing channels in other cultural regions.
>
> (Hopkinson & Blois, 2014, p. 142)

Looking at this issue from the wider geopolitical perspective (Khanna, 2019), future research on power should employ a more pluralistic cultural understanding of power, as current Western-oriented research on power in business relationships does not correspond well with the ongoing trend of balancing power between several nations, including in particular the USA and China.

1.1.5 Summary

Although our review on power in business relationships shows the complexity of this construct and raises some important questions without providing answers, our intention was not to overcomplicate issues related to power so much as to make them unresolvable. In contrast, we actually call for more research on power incorporating various theoretical and methodological approaches. We also call for more research incorporating explicit assumptions of what power is and confronting it with other approaches. This is important as it will reveal any research limitations, which to date has rarely been the case. The justification for more research on power in business relationships comes not only from the limitations of existing empirical works, but also from the power-related trends observed in international supply chains and marketing channels, which illustrate the importance of power in inter-firm relationships. In general, business practice is providing more and more evidence for the significant shifts occurring in value chains, where previously dominated companies employ certain specific capabilities to improve their positions and acquire access to a bigger slice of the relationship pie. These instances go beyond the rise of Chinese companies to include companies originating in smaller countries in the process of transformation (e.g. Bai et al., 2021; Ciszewska-Mlinarič et al., 2020; Mitręga et al., 2021). It would be extremely interesting to see how these shifts correspond with shifts in multifaceted power, especially how they correspond with power in terms of the cultural values that dominate international value chains.

1.2 Power-related tactics in asymmetrical buyer-supplier relationships

1.2.1 Introduction

Although power asymmetry in dyadic buyer-supplier relationships affects the value of the relationship from the perspective of both actors (Liu et al., 2018), the main focus of the literature is on the impact of power asymmetry on the weaker party to the relationship and its response to this (e.g. Lacoste & Johnsen, 2015; Nyaga et al., 2013; Siemieniako & Mitręga, 2018a). In this subsection, we follow the literature on the power-related tactics of weaker suppliers in their relationship with dominant buyers (e.g. Benton & Maloni, 2005; Cowan et al., 2015; Lacoste & Johnson, 2015; Pérez & Cambra-Fierro, 2015).

The purpose of this subsection is to address several research questions. 1) What are the motivations for the weaker side of the relationship to undertake power-related tactics? 2) What actions does the weaker supplier in the relationship take with respect to improving its power position in order to increase value from the relationship with stronger buyers? 3) Which of these tactics are intentional and which are non-intentional (these issues are discussed in more detail in subsection 2.1.) with regard to improving their power position? 4) How does power asymmetry/symmetry positively or negatively affect the relationship outcome and the performance of the weaker suppliers and dominant buyers? To answer these questions, we reviewed selected articles, including a focus on an in-depth analysis of Siemieniako and Mitręga's (2018a) study.

1.2.2   The risks posed to the weaker party by asymmetric power relations as a determinant of undertaking power-related tactics

Business-to-business literature shows the different approaches adopted by weaker suppliers to address the issue of power asymmetry in business relationships, as discussed in subsection 1.1. Part of the literature focuses on showing the rather negative impact of power asymmetry in buyer-supplier relationships (e.g. Hingley et al., 2015; Rokkan & Haughland, 2002; Ulrich & Barney, 1984; Wolfe & McGinn, 2005), especially substantial power asymmetry (Nyaga et al., 2013) on the value obtained from the relationship by the weaker side. Various strategies and tactics are revealed from the perspective of the weaker party to the relationship (Cowan et al., 2015; Lacoste & Johnson, 2015; Liu et al., 2018; Pérez & Cambra-Fierro, 2015). From the other side, it is not so obvious as there is also a large portion of research which shows that even in situations of substantial power asymmetry, buyer-supplier relationships can be rewarding for weaker sides that do not pursue action to improve their power position (Caniëls et al., 2018; Caniëls & Gelderman, 2007; Clemens & Douglas, 2006; Hingley, 2005; Xuan et al., 2020).

Important factors are also indicated that relate to the strategy of the weaker party in the relationship. For example, changes in the external environment can be seen as an opportunity to improve the power position of the weaker party (Cheung et al., 2010), e.g. with regards to innovative performance (Wang, 2011). The choice of strategic objectives (e.g. entering international markets with their own product, increasing profit margins) may involve seeking to improve power in relationships with dominant buyers (Siemieniako & Mitręga, 2018a; Lacoste & Johnsen, 2015). Cultural issues (Horak & Long, 2018; Zeng et al., 2020) on the weaker party's side, including the style

of doing business with stronger buyers (e.g. the personal reluctance of own-
ers to increase dependency on a single buyer, or the culturally determined
reluctance to undertake coercive activities on the part of large buyers), are
also important as an influencing factor on the approach of the weaker party to
the relationship to power-related tactics. A significant motivator for weaker
suppliers to undertake power-related tactics aimed at improving their power
position may be the limited learning benefits available after many years in
a relationship with a large customer (see: Lin et al., 2017; Pérez & Cambra-
Fierro, 2015). A long-standing relationship with a dominant customer may
also lead to relationship embedding (Siemieniako & Mitręga, 2018a; Soontornthum et al., 2020) and reduced opportunities to acquire new customers
due to value misalignment with new customer requirements.

As Siemieniako and Mitręga (2018a) stated, power asymmetry is a likely
element of every relationship between selling and buying companies, but the
weaker side should pro-actively anticipate associated risks by improving its
power position in a non-coercive way. The aim of weaker suppliers' power-
related tactics is to maximise the value from relationships with large buyers
and increase suppliers' performance, not just to improve their power position.

1.2.3 Power-related tactics of weaker suppliers in asymmetrical relationships

There is growing interest in the idea that power structure dynamics in business dyads proceeds not only according to a "natural cycle", including situational factors independent of the actors, but that such dynamics can be
intentionally leveraged vis-à-vis actors' activities to achieve greater benefits
from the relationship (Cox et al., 2004; Siemieniako & Mitręga, 2018b).
Lacoste and Johnsen (2015) refer to "countervailing power" in their study,
finding that "Suppliers will do their utmost to shift the balance of power
in their favour and decrease the power asymmetry" (p. 231). The Lacoste
and Johnsen (2015) study shows that a specific product category (i.e. quasi-
commodity products) can be moved from the leverage quadrant (Kraljic,
1983), in which the buyer is the dominant party, towards the strategic quadrant, where the power between the partners is balanced. In their conceptual
work, Cowan et al. (2015) proposed practices that a weaker supplier can
use in relationships with stronger buyers so as to achieve greater benefits
from such relationships. These are as follows: investment in development
or acquisition of resources and competencies, working to reduce competition, becoming indispensable, lowering barriers, working together to reach
a common goal and developing a team mentality.

Empirical works on power-related tactics have also emerged. In Lacoste
and Johnsen's (2015) research, the shift of power between the exchange

partners is caused by an increased level of services delivered by supplier, leading to increased total value perceived by the customer. Pérez and Cambra-Fierro (2015) conducted case studies related to power tactics and identified the following tactics: learning to work together, informal communication and committed champions, specific investments/specialisation on the supplier side, taking a long-term perspective and focusing on a limited number of value-creating relationships.

It is worth mentioning that in Lacoste and Johnsen's (2015) case study, a supplier's offer of an increased level of service to a more powerful buyer was intentional from the perspective of improving the supplier's power position in the relationship. Interestingly, the work of Cowan et al. (2015), as well as Pérez and Cambra-Fierro (2015), did not categorise whether the power-related tactics were intentional with respect to changing the power position, or non-purposeful and oriented more towards business goals, while still improving the power position of the weaker party.

Siemieniako and Mitręga (2018a) continued the research strand into power-related tactics and concluded from their case studies that four general tactics are used by weaker suppliers to deal with powerful business buyers: orientation towards product specialisation, making extraordinary efforts, learning to work together and maintaining a reasonable share of customer sales. They noted 15 various power-related tactics, which were grouped within four general tactics. These 15 tactics were related to non-mediated power only (i.e. soft power). Siemieniako and Mitręga (2018a) indicated only four specific tactics as intentional, while 11 were found to be non-intentional in relation to improving the supplier's power position (see Table 1.2.). Most of the specific tactics related to orientation towards the general tactic of product specialisation were identified as intentional tactics, namely: acquiring other customers on the basis of similarity with the existing customer, learning in a narrow range of activity and aiming to be the sole supplier of a specific product for the customer. One more intentional tactic (i.e. expanding supplier participation in the value chain) was grouped with three other non-intentional tactics under the general tactic of maintaining a reasonable share of sales to the dominant customer. The other specific tactics were grouped under general tactics: taking extraordinary efforts and learning to work together were described within the case studies as non-intentional tactics related to improvement of the weaker supplier's power position, although still with a bearing on improvement of non-mediated power. As Siemieniako and Mitręga (2018a) found in their research, all of the power-related tactics adopted by weaker suppliers seem to help the companies in strengthening their position in supply chains and gaining relationship benefits.

As Siemieniako and Mitręga (2018a) found, although these typologies were not entirely the same, they all suggested that countervailing practices

Table 1.2 Intentional and non-intentional tactics regarding improvement of a weaker supplier's power position

Weaker supplier's general tactics	Weaker supplier's detailed tactics	Intentional tactics regarding improvement of supplier's power position (Yes/No)
1. Taking extraordinary efforts	1.1. The role of the parent company in motivating suppliers	No
	1.2. Fulfilling prerequisites for being chosen by the powerful customer	No
	1.3. Development of specific resources and competencies	No
	1.4. Becoming more open in information sharing	No
2. Orientation toward product specialisation	2.1. Focusing on a limited number of value-creating relationships	No
	2.2. Acquiring other customers on the basis of similarity with the existing one	Yes
	2.3. Learning in a narrow range of activity	Yes
	2.4. Building a position as the buyer's sole supplier of a specific product	Yes
3. Learning to work together	3.1. Implementing a Key Account Management position	No
	3.2. Excellence in communication on an organisational and personal level	No
	3.3. Implementing measurement procedures to keep the customer well informed	No
	3.4. Developing a team mentality at the inter-firm operational level	No
4. Maintaining a reasonable share of sales to the dominant customer	4.1. Extending supplier core capabilities beyond the initial position within the value chain	Yes
	4.2. Mitigating the risk of bankruptcy	No
	4.3. Using the dominant customer as a reference to acquire other customers	No

Source: Based on Siemieniako and Mitręga (2018a)

(Lacoste & Johnsen, 2015) are usually initiated by the weaker side in relationships where power asymmetry is substantial. The empirical works presented above illustrate that practices oriented toward power asymmetry are based rather on non-mediated power sources, e.g. expert power and referent power (French & Raven, 1959). In general, the weaker business partner makes efforts to improve its competences and image in the relationship with the dominating partner, and at the same time revise its position within the supply chain. Thus, it seems that the Kraljic matrix (1983) can to some extent be applied to the supplier's business. This is because there is growing evidence that suppliers may effectively handle their vulnerability with regard to strategic customers by applying similar tactics to those that industrial buyers used to apply towards their supply base (e.g. exploiting expert power position and diversifying). However, in contrast to the strategies suggested for purchasing managers, sales managers in supplier companies should instead use non-mediated power tactics, as these tactics were found to work effectively for them.

Power-related research (Siemieniako & Mitręga, 2018b) in asymmetrical buyer-supplier relationships also illustrates that the power shift between business partners is additionally influenced by the nature of the business relationship itself (i.e. the relationship development cycle and its multiple stages), as well as the general business environment (e.g. the competitive situation on the buying company's market, or the general business climate) (Cheung et al., 2010). We have used the concept of contextual events (Makkonen et al., 2012) to describe such external factors and their influence on the focal relationship (see subsection 2.1.)

1.2.4   Two-sided power-related tactics in buyer-supplier asymmetrical relationships

Although dyadic research on power-related tactics in buyer-supplier relationships (e.g. Cuevas et al., 2015; Lacoste & Johnsen, 2015; Nyaga et al., 2013; Siemieniako & Mitręga, 2018a), has focused on improvement of the weaker supplier's power position, it has also revealed that this is not a one-sided process. Siemieniako and Mitręga (2018a) identified tactics not only related to the power of weaker suppliers (see Table 1.2), but also power-related tactics used by dominant buyers, very often connected with supplier tactics in terms of initiating certain actions or as a reaction to actions taken by the other side of the relationship. Their dyadic case studies involved interviews with supplier and buyer representatives on power-related tactics with regard to the impact of these tactics on the implications for relationship benefits and overall performance. Table 1.3 shows all four intentional supplier tactics (see Table 1.2) used to improve the power position and its

Table 1.3 Weaker suppliers' tactics and their consequences for the relationship with dominant buyers

Weaker suppliers' tactics	Consequences for the relationship	Consequences for suppliers' performance
Intentional tactics to improve suppliers' power (focal events)		
- Acquiring other customers on the basis of similarity with the existing one, through improving the suppliers credibility on the market (*copied from Table 1.2, 2.2*)	- Aligning the supplier image with a benchmarked MNC buyer attracts interest from other buyers - Less dependence on the buyer	- More balanced revenue and annual order fluctuation - Reduced risk of bankruptcy due to the possibility of losing a key customer
- Learning in a narrow range of activity (*copied from Table 1.2, 2.3*)	- The buyer recognised that the supplier has greater expertise in key operations and management	- Improved supplier operations and expansion of their strategic horizons
- Building a position as the buyer's sole supplier of a specific product (*copied from Table 1.2, 2.4*)	- The buyer recognised the supplier's position as irreplaceable because in the short term the buyer had no other alternative	- More stable financial planning and minimised risk of losing the buyer
- Extending supplier core capabilities beyond the initial position within the value chain (*copied from Table 1.2, 4.1*)	- The buyer perceived an increased level of supplier expertise in the extended value chain - Increased supplier attractiveness and better bargaining conditions for new customers	- Improved supplier sales performance due to increased service to the customer
Suppliers' power use tactics		
- Requiring a higher sales margin from the buyer (*associated with 2.4, Table 1.2*)	- Loss of position as the sole supplier to a specific buyer caused by an unexpected decline in power	- Deterioration of sales performance of a specific product line supplied to the buyer by only one supplier - Periodic lack of enquiries from the buyer for new products due to the use of power by the supplier

Source: Based on Siemieniako and Mitręga (2018a)

implications for relationship benefits and supplier performance. One example of the use of power on the supplier side is also identified. Table 1.4 presents dominant buyers' intentional power-related tactics and examples of the exercising of power.

As presented in Tables 1.3 and 1.4, both weaker suppliers and stronger buyers took various intentional activities within the relationship overall to

Table 1.4 Dominant buyers' tactics and their consequences for the relationship with weaker suppliers

Dominant buyers' tactics	Consequences for the relationship	Consequences for buyers' performance
Intentional tactics to improve buyers' power (focal events)		
- Diversifying the supplier base *(associated with all tactics, Table 1.2)*	- Reduced reliance on troublesome suppliers	- Poorer financial results
- Inviting suppliers into initiatives requiring more expertise, e.g. new product development *(associated with 2.3, Table 1.2)*	- Suppliers perceived their knowledge limitations with regard to supplier tactics	- Reduction in the buyer's indirect costs due to an increase in the scope of services provided by the same supplier
Buyers' power using tactics		
- Using contractual advantage in relation to mediated types of power *(associated with 2.3, Table 1.2)*	- Pressure from the supplier for a more balanced contractual arrangement - Limited trust on the part of the supplier	- Increased purchasing efficiencies and supplier controllability
- Requiring the supplier to make costly operational adjustments under threat of reduced procurement by the buyer *(associated with general tactic 1, Table 1.2)*	- Pressure from the supplier to share operational alignment costs - Improved partnership in the relationship due to the buyer agreeing to share 50% of the costs	- Reduction of direct costs for the buyer
- Requiring the supplier to invest in improvement of competencies under threat of limiting the scope of cooperation *(associated with 1.3, Table 1.2)*	- The participatory approach to cost-benefit sharing had the effect (rather long-term) of increasing the tendency to balance non-mediated power in the relationship	- Improved level of value delivery by the supplier

Source: Based on Siemieniako and Mitręga (2018a)

reinforce their own power position, as in the studies by Lacoste and Johnsen (2015) and Cowan et al. (2015). Interestingly, the stronger buyers also took action to improve the weaker side's power position in order to increase the value from the relationship. This is clearly visible in the dominant buyers' reactions (Table 1.3, "Consequences for the relationship" column), for instance in their recognition that the supplier has greater expertise in key operations and management as a result of the supplier's tactics, namely: learning management skills from the buyer. This supports the concept of joint learning capacity, which is crucial in justifying OEM suppliers' asset specific investments (Lin et al., 2017).

Not surprisingly, the exercising of power is mainly carried out by dominant buyers (Table 1.4), which is in line with research to date showing that power is mainly exercised by the stronger partners in business relationships (e.g. Buchanan, 1992; Rindt & Mouzas, 2015). An example is also presented of the use of power on the weaker supplier side (Table 1.3), which resulted in negative consequences in the relationship with the dominant buyer and negative outcomes for the supplier. The results presented in Tables 1.3 and 1.4 are consistent with the literature, and confirm that the use of coercive power can be detrimental to the relationship, and can trigger the use of coercive practices by the other party to the relationship. Conversely, non-coercive tactics are treated positively in the literature in terms of the benefits to the relationship. Similarly, non-coercive tactics elicit non-coercive practices from the other relationship partner (Frazier & Rody, 1991; Johnson et al., 1993; Siemieniako & Mitręga, 2018a, 2018b).

1.2.5 *Summary*

Consequently, improvement of the power position should be treated as a long-term management process aimed at getting closer to a "relationship golden mean" within the constraints of the wider relational structures that surround a business dyad (Siemieniako & Mitręga, 2018b). The aim of "ideal" power symmetry would appear to be an abstract concept in business practice, not only because it may be economically ineffective, but also due to the complexity of relationship power itself and the many sources of power, i.e. dominance in one power source can be offset by being dominated with regard to another power source. Power practices should not strive for "perfect" power symmetry, not least because business partners are usually very different and these differences are needed to obtain benefits from the relationship, e.g. through complementarities (Dyer & Singh, 1998). In a similar vein, a study by Cox et al. (2004), concluded that in achieving "ideal" performance outcomes in business relationships, attention should be paid to finding an appropriate level of interdependence between the buyer and seller. At the same time, it can be seen that power practices are not simply abstract constructs, but that they contribute to business relationships without harming the relationships themselves (Lacoste & Johnsen, 2015; Johnsen & Lacoste, 2016; Pérez & Cambra-Fierro, 2015; Siemieniako & Mitręga, 2018a, 2018b).

1.3 References

Bai, W., Johanson, M., Oliveira, L., & Ratajczak-Mrozek, M. (2021). The role of business and social networks in the effectual internationalization: Insights from emerging market SMEs. *Journal of Business Research*, 129, 96–109.

Blois, K. (2010). The legitimacy of power in business-to-business relationships. *Marketing Theory*, 10(2), 161–172.

Bourdieu, P. (1979). Symbolic power. *Critique of Anthropology*, 4(13–14), 77–85.

Bourdieu, P. (1989). Social space and symbolic power. *Sociological Theory*, 7(1), 14–25.

Boyle, B., Dwyer, F. R., Robicheaux, R. A., & Simpson, J. T. (1992). Influence strategies in marketing channels: Measures and use in different relationship structures. *Journal of Marketing Research*, 29(4), 462–473.

Chang, K. H., & Huang, H. F. (2012). Using influence strategies to advance supplier delivery flexibility: The moderating roles of trust and shared vision. *Industrial Marketing Management*, 41(5), 849–860.

Cheung, M. S., Myers, M. B., & Mentzer, J. T. (2010). Does relationship learning lead to relationship value? A cross-national supply chain investigation. *Journal of Operations Management*, 28(6), 472–487.

Ciszewska-Mlinarič, M., Wójcik, P., & Obłój, K. (2020). Learning dynamics of rapidly internationalizing venture: Beyond the early stage of international growth in a CEE context. *Journal of Business Research*, 108, 450–465.

Cowan, K., Paswan, A. K., & Van Steenburg, E. (2015). When inter-firm relationship benefits mitigate power asymmetry. *Industrial Marketing Management*, 48, 140–148.

Czernek-Marszałek, K. (2020). The overembeddedness impact on tourism cooperation. *Annals of Tourism Research*, 81, 102852.

Dyer, J. H., & Singh, H. (1998). The relational view: Cooperative strategy and sources of interorganisational competitive advantage. *The Academy of Management Review*, 23(4), 660–679.

Dyer, J. H., Singh, H., & Kale, P. (2008). Splitting the pie: Rent distribution in alliances and networks. *Managerial and Decision Economics*, 29(2–3), 137–148.

Emerson, R. M. (1962). Power-dependence relations. *American Sociological Review*, 31–41.

Foucault, M. (1977). *Discipline and punish: The birth of the prison*. New York: Random House.

Frazier, G. L., & Rody, R. C. (1991). The use of influence strategies in interfirm relationships in industrial product channels. *The Journal of Marketing*, 52–69.

Frazier, G. L., & Summers, J. O. (1984). Interfirm influence strategies and their application within distribution channels. *Journal of Marketing*, 48(3), 43–55.

French, J. R. P., & Raven, B. (1959). *The bases of social power*. Classics of organisation theory, 7.

Fu, S., Zhan, Y., Ouyang, J., Ding, Y., Tan, K. H., & Fu, L. (2021). Power, supply chain integration and quality performance of agricultural products: Evidence from contract farming in China. *Production Planning & Control*, 32(13), 1119–1135.

Gassenheimer, J. B., & Ramsey, R. (1994). The impact of dependence on dealer satisfaction: A comparison of reseller-supplier relationships. *Journal of Retailing*, 70(3), 253–266.

Gaventa, J. (2001). *Power after Lukes: A review of the literature*. Brighton: Institute of Development Studies.

Geyskens, I., Steenkamp, J. B. E. M., & Kumar, N. (1999). A meta-analysis of satisfaction in marketing channel relationships. *Journal of marketing Research*, 36(2), 223–238.

Gramsci, A. (1971). *Selections from the prison notebooks of Antonio Gramsci*. New York: International Publishers.

Hagedoorn, J., & Frankort, H. T. W. (2008). The gloomy side of embeddedness: The effects of overembeddedness on inter-firm partnership formation. *Advances in Strategic Management*, 25, 503–530.

Håkansson, H. (1982). *International marketing and purchasing of industrial goods: An interaction approach*. England: Chichester.

Herbig, P. (1996). *Market signalling: A review*. Management Decision.

Hopkinson, G. C., & Blois, K. (2014). Power-base research in marketing channels: A narrative review. *International Journal of Management Reviews*, 16(2), 131–149.

Horak, S., & Long, C. P. (2018). Dissolving the paradox: Toward a Yin–Yang perspective on the power and trust antagonism in collaborative business relationships. *Supply Chain Management: An International Journal*, 23(6), 573–590.

Huo, B., Tian, M., Tian, Y., & Zhang, Q. (2019). The dilemma of inter-organizational relationships: Dependence, use of power and their impacts on opportunism. *International Journal of Operations & Production Management*, 39(1), 2–23.

Jain, M., Khalil, S., Johnston, W. J., & Cheng, J. M. S. (2014). The performance implications of power–trust relationship: The moderating role of commitment in the supplier–retailer relationship. *Industrial Marketing Management*, 43(2), 312–321.

Johnsen, R. E., Lacoste, S., & Meehan, J. (2020). Hegemony in asymmetric customer-supplier relationships. *Industrial Marketing Management*, 87, 63–75.

Johnson, J. L., Sakano, T., Cote, J. A., & Onzo, N. (1993). The exercise of inter-firm power and its repercussions in US-Japanese channel relationships. *Journal of Marketing*, 57(2), 1–10.

Khanna, P. (2019). *The future is Asian*. Simon and Schuster.

Kubacki, K., Siemieniako, D., & Brennan, L. (2020). Building positive resilience through vulnerability analysis. *Journal of Social Marketing*, 10(4), 471–488.

Lacoste, S., & Johnsen, R. E. (2015). Supplier–customer relationships: A case study of power dynamic. *Journal of Purchasing and Supply Management*, 21(4), 229–240.

Lai, C. S. (2007). The effects of influence strategies on dealer satisfaction and performance in Taiwan's motor industr. *Industrial Marketing Management*, 36(4), 518–527.

Lee, D. Y. (2001). Power, conflict and satisfaction in IJV supplier–Chinese distributor channels. *Journal of Business Research*, 52(2), 149–160.

Lin, C. W., Wu, L. Y., & Chiou, J. S. (2017). The use of asset specific investments to increase customer dependence: A study of OEM suppliers. *Industrial Marketing Management*, 67, 174–184.

Low, W. S., & Li, C. T. (2019). Power advantage: Antecedents and consequences in supplier–retailer relationships. *Journal of Business & Industrial Marketing*, 34(6), 1323–1338.

Makkonen, H., Siemieniako, D., & Mitręga, M. (2021). Structural and behavioural power dynamics in buyer-supplier relationships: A perceptions-based framework and a research agenda. *Technology Analysis & Strategic Management*, 1–15.

Manaresi, A., & Uncles, M. (1995). *Retail franchising in Britain and Italy*. International Retailing: Trends and Strategies, Pitman, London, 151–167.

Mishra, M., & Banerjee, M. (2019). Non-coercive influence: Scale development and validation based on resource and relational paradigms. *Journal of Purchasing and Supply Management*, 25(3), 100498.

Mitręga, M., & Choi, T. M. (2021). How small-and-medium transportation companies handle asymmetric customer relationships under COVID-19 pandemic: A multi-method study. *Transportation Research Part E: Logistics and Transportation Review*, 148, 102249.

Mitrega, M., Siemieniako, D., Makkonen, H., Kubacki, K., & Bresciani, S. (2021). Versatile capabilities for growth in the context of transforming countries: Evidence from Polish manufacturing companies. *Journal of Business Research*, 134, 156–170.

Mora-Monge, C., Quesada, G., Gonzalez, M. E., & Davis, J. M. (2019). Trust, power and supply chain integration in Web-enabled supply chains. *Supply Chain Management: An International Journal*.

Oukes, T., von Raesfeld, A. & Groen, A. (2019). Power in a startup's relationships with its established partners: Interactions between structural and behavioural power. *Industrial Marketing Management*, 80, 68–83.

Pérez, L., & Cambra-Fierro, J. (2015). Learning to work in asymmetric relationships: Insights from the computer software industry. *Supply Chain Management: An International Journal*, 20(1), 1–10.

Pfefer, J., & Salancik, G. (1978). *The external control of organizations*. New York: Harper and Row.

Pfeffer, J. (1987). A resource dependence perspective on intercorporate relations. In M. S. Mizruchi & M. Schwartz (Eds.), *Intercorporate relations: The structural analysis of business*. Cambridge, MA: Cambridge University Press.

Pulles, N. J., Veldman, J., Schiele, H., & Sierksma, H. (2014). Pressure or pamper? The effects of power and trust dimensions on supplier resource allocation. *Journal of Supply Chain Management*, 50(3), 16–36.

Randall, W. S., Gibson, B. J., Defee, C. C., & Williams, B. D. (2011). Retail supply chain management: Key priorities and practices. *The International Journal of Logistics Management*.

Ratajczak-Mrozek, M. (2017). *Network embeddedness, examining the effect on business performance and internationalization.* Cham, Switzerland: Palgrave Macmillan.

Raven, B. H. (1965). Social influence and power. In I. D. Steiner & M. Fishbein (Eds.), *Current studies in social psychology.* New York: Holt, Rinehart, Winston.

Raven, B. H. (1992). A power/interaction model of interpersonal influence: French and Raven thirty years later. *Journal of Social Behavior & Personality.*

Scheer, L. K., Kumar, N., & Steenkamp, J. B. E. M. (2003). Reactions to perceived inequity in US and Dutch interorganisational relationships. *Academy of Management Journal,* 46(3), 303–316.

Siemieniako, D., & Kaliszewski, P. (2022). Factors influencing structural power dynamics in buyer-supplier relationships: A power sources framework and application of the critical incident technique. *Oeconomia Copernicana* (in press).

Siemieniako, D., Makkonen, H., & Mitręga, M. (2021). *Power mechanism capabilities of value co-creation within and outside buyer-supplier international relationship: A longitudinal study on power dynamics.* Online CBIM 2021 International Conference: Challenges and Opportunities for Increasing Turbulent Times in Business Markets, Georgia State University, Atlanta, USA, 22–24.06.2021.

Siemieniako, D., & Mitręga, M. (2018a). Improving power position with regard to non-mediated power sources: The supplier's perspective. *Industrial Marketing Management,* 70, 90–100.

Siemieniako, D., & Mitręga, M. (2018b). *Is it good to balance power in a buyer-seller "business marriage" and how it happens?* 34th IMP Conference: From Business to Research and Back Again, Kedge Business School, Marseille Campus, Marseille, France 4–7.09.2018. Available at: www.impgroup.org/paper_view.php?viewPaper=9889 [data of access: 2021.11.12].

Siemieniako, D., & Mitręga, M. (2019). *Yesterday is gone, tomorrow has not yet come: Exploring power shifts in buyer-seller business relationships.* 35th IMP Conference: Relationships Interactions and Networks in competitive environment, IESEG School of Management, Paris, France, 27–30.08.2019. Available at: www.impgroup.org/paper_view.php?viewPaper=11117 [data of access: 2021.11.12].

Soontornthum, T., Cui, L., Lu, V. N., & Su, J. (2020). Enabling SMEs' learning from global value chains: Linking the logic of power and the logic of embeddedness of interfirm relations. *Management International Review,* 60(4), 543–571.

Vos, F. G. S., Van der Lelij, R., Schiele, H., & Praas, N. H. J. (2021). Mediating the impact of power on supplier satisfaction: Do buyer status and relational conflict matter? *International Journal of Production Economics,* 239, 108168.

Wang, C. H. (2011). The moderating role of power asymmetry on the relationships between alliance and innovative performance in the high-tech industry. *Technological Forecasting and Social Change,* 78(7), 1268–1279.

Wilkinson, I., & Kipnis, D. (1978). Interfirm use of power. *Journal of Applied Psychology,* 63(3), 315.

Xuan, P. A. N., Shuwei, Z. A. N. G., Yiyang, H. U., & Jinyang, L. I. U. (2020). Identifying the positive sides of power use between (in) congruence in distributive fairness perception and supplier-buyer relationship quality. *Industrial Marketing Management,* 91, 362–372.

Yeung, J. H. Y., Selen, W., Zhang, M., & Huo, B. (2009). The effects of trust and coercive power on supplier integration. *International Journal of Production Economics*, 120(1), 66–78.

Zadykowicz, A., Chmielewski, K., & Siemieniako, D. (2020). Proactive customer orientation and joint learning capabilities in collaborative machine to machine innovation technology development: The case study of automotive equipment manufacturer. *Oeconomia Copernicana*, 11(3), 415–423.

Zeng, F., Ye, Q., Dong, M. C., Huang, Z., & Liu, Z. (2020). Legitimizing actions in dependence-asymmetry relationships: A comparison between Chinese and Western firms. *Industrial Marketing Management*, 88, 163–172.

Zhang, Q., Pan, J., Xu, D., & Feng, T. (2020). Balancing coercive and non-coercive powers to enhance green supplier integration: Do relationship commitment and closeness matter? *Supply Chain Management: An International Journal*, 25(6), 637–653.

2 Relationship power dynamics as a focus of scientific research and an area for business practice implications

2.1 Advancing the study of power dynamics in business relationships: introducing a power dynamics canvas and narrative approach

2.1.1 Introduction

Burrell and Morgan (1979) presented their classic division of sociological paradigms along the dimensions of subjective-objective and stability-change. The former refers to assumptions on human nature, ontology, epistemology and methodology, and the latter to assumptions on the nature of society/organisation. These dimensions provide a matrix of four archetypes of sociological paradigms; "radical humanist", "radical structuralist", "interpretive" and "functionalist". These broad, overarching paradigms resonate well with research streams on power in business relationships, and are clearly manifested in both theoretical conceptualisations as well as the research methods employed in extant power dynamics research.

The main purpose of this chapter is to capture the multifaceted nature of power dynamics in business relationships and introduce a narrative approach as a means for its empirical study. The consideration in the next section is two-fold. The first section discusses the concept of power and synthesises a power dynamics canvas. The second section introduces the narrative approach, while the third discusses the opportunities for its use in the study of power dynamics in business relationships. Finally, the use of the power dynamics canvas and narrative approach in further research is concluded in section three.

2.1.2 Conceptualising power dynamics in business relationships: a power dynamics canvas

For a long time, the literature has defined power as a function of the dependency between parties (see Etgar, 1976; Meehan & Wright, 2011). Early work on power (Dahl, 1957; Emerson, 1962) focused on social exchange and

DOI: 10.4324/9781003095934-3

inter-individual relationships within groups and organisations. However, as the context of the focus spreads from the inter-individual to the inter-organisational context, the issue of power is becoming ever more multi-dimensional and intertwined with various temporal (past-present-future) and hierarchical dimensions (individual, organisation, relationship) that are inherent features of business relationships (see e.g. Makkonen & Olkkonen, 2017). This multiplicity produces a variety of viewpoints on power, some rigid and operating on one dimension, for example, focusing on individuals (Wilson, 2000) or organisations (e.g. Sanderson, 2004) as the sources of power, while other approaches are more inclusive and synthesise individual, organisational and relationship levels into overarching accounts of power (see Meehan & Wright, 2011). In addition to variety in the levels of analysis, the literature identifies the relativistic nature of the concept of power: inter-firm power is about the objective properties of a powerful party, i.e. the power source, as well as its perception by the weaker party i.e. the power target (see Johnsen et al., 2020; Lacoste & Johnsen, 2015; Oukes et al., 2019).

One classification widely elaborated in the literature, are the power base dimensions of mediated and non-mediated power (Benton & Maloni, 2005; Maloni & Benton, 2000). Mediated power refers to the potential for the power source to engage in explicit actions i.e. the use of coercive, legitimate or reward power, to draw on the extrinsic motivation of the power target to comply with the requests of the power source (Brown et al., 1995). Non-mediated power is not associated with explicit actions, but refers to elements linked to the power source that the power target values. Respectively, the power target aims to be associated with the power source in terms of expert, referent and informational forms of power, and is thus intrinsically motivated to comply with the requests of the power source (Zhao et al., 2008; Zadykowicz et al., 2020). In this regard, the power target believes in gains from the collaboration and thus voluntarily gives control to the more powerful party. Furthermore, previous literature describes mediated power as negative and short-term oriented, while non-mediated power is seen as positive and long-term oriented (Benton & Maloni, 2005; Handley & Benton, 2012; Brown et al., 1995).

Power asymmetry, that is an imbalance in the division of power between the buyer and supplier (Munksgaard et al., 2015), has been linked in the literature to both negative and positive consequences. The negative side underlines the harmful effects of power asymmetry in B2B relationships, such as: neglect of the low-power party by the high-power party (Wolfe & McGinn, 2005), the limited effectiveness of joint initiatives (Pfeffer & Salanick, 1978; Ulrich & Barney, 1984), conflicts and a repressive atmosphere (Ojansivu et al., 2013), and low stability and poor relationship outcomes (see Hingley et al., 2015; Rokkan & Haughland, 2002). However, positively oriented writings consider power asymmetry to be a stabilising force that clarifies the role structure and decision-making in the relationship (see Hingley, 2005; Caniëls & Gelderman, 2007; Clemens & Douglas, 2006; Xuan et al., 2020). All in all, evaluation of the consequences of power asymmetry is difficult due to its multifaceted nature, as well as the fact that power asymmetry does not necessarily mean extensive use of power but rather the option to use power, which the power source may decide not to implement in practice (see Nyaga et al., 2013).

In general, there are different dynamics in buyer-supplier relationships (e.g. Shamsollahi et al., 2020). In this section, we adopt a dynamic view on power, according to which power, as well as power asymmetry, are to be understood in conjunction with the relationship and its role among the actors' other relationships (Cowan et al., 2015, p. 146). Power dynamics can be intentionally leveraged vis-à-vis actors' attempts to build countervailing power and influence the distribution of power in the relationship (see Cox et al., 2004; Lacoste & Johnsen, 2015; Siemieniako & Mitręga, 2018a). In addition to explicit countervailing power actions, power dynamics may be caused by developments, actions and events within and outside the focal relationship. This view is widely acknowledged in research on industrial relationships and purchasing, where power is treated as a common, complex, dynamic phenomenon, strongly based on the perspective of business partners and embedded within a set of direct and indirect influences (Lacoste & Blois, 2015). In this regard, the framework below in Figure 2.1,

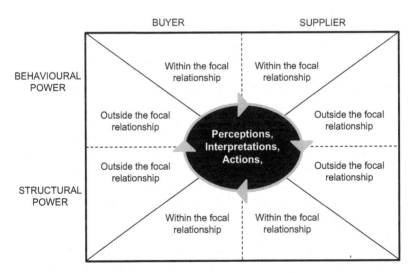

Figure 2.1 Power dynamics canvas

the power dynamics canvas, defines power dynamics as emergent products of relationship development, out of reach of the direct management actions of a single relationship actor (Håkansson & Ford, 2002).

To sum up, the framework in Figure 2.1 features a power dynamics canvas which defines power dynamics as changes in the division of power between the parties of the buyer and supplier in terms of behavioural and structural power. Perceptions, interpretations and actions are placed in the central panel i.e. activities that occur within and outside the focal relationship. Previous research largely emphasised the structural issue of power dynamics, while perspectives on behavioural power dynamics, i.e. dynamics in power use, were ignored. To achieve a balanced approach, the framework defines power dynamics as changes in both behavioural and structural power. To complement the idea of intentional, countervailing power actions dominant in the literature (see e.g. Oukes et al., 2019), the framework adopts a more general approach in considering actions and events within and outside the focal relationship as being potential sources of power dynamics that alter the division or asymmetry of power in the relationship. The different sections of the canvas may emphasise as the relationship develops further or per how the parties interpret, perceive and act upon different elements within and outside the relationship regarding structural and behavioural power. The perceptions and interpretations of key individuals mediate the influence of such purposeful and non-purposeful events and actions into power (see Makkonen et al., 2012). The following section introduces a narrative approach for studying power dynamics in business relationships.

2.1.3 *Applying the narrative approach to the study of power dynamics in business relationships*

The narrative approach focuses on producing and analysing narratives: entities follow a plot in which activities, events, actors, motives and context form a unified whole that progresses in a temporal story structure (Polkinghorne, 1995; Elliott, 2005). A narrative is constructed by a narrator from their subjective perspective and orientation (Elliott, 2005; Pentland, 1999). As the number of elements that fit into a communicative story is restricted, the narrator chooses, consciously or unconsciously, the configuration of narrative elements and their emphasis. However, this subjectivity is not to be interpreted as a contamination of the truth, but as a means to understand one's viewpoint and perceptions, as well as interpretations of the chain of events and the functioning mechanisms. In other words, a narrative reveals causal pathways i.e. how events relate to each other and manifest the context (Elliot, 2005) as perceived and communicated by the narrator (Makkonen et al., 2012). Such a story is relatively easy to understand and compare with other narratives or communicate in actual discussion with other narrators, as stories comprise a natural means of communication and humans have narrative cognition by nature (Bruner, 1986). Such narrative cognition is not restricted to concepts or theoretical paradigms, i.e. paradigmatic cognition, and thus offers a more neutral approach for grasping real-life phenomena (Ricoeur, 1984) without the primary aim being that of conceptual reduction (see Bartel & Garud, 2009).

Makkonen et al. (2012) discuss the narrative approach for the purposes of network process research. They make a distinction between informant, researcher, community and research community narratives. Informant narratives refer to stories formed of data from individual informants, for example through interviews or other means of data gathering that convey the tone of the informants in a narrative form (Flick, 2002). Researcher narratives refer to researcher constructed narratives composed of individual sets of data. Informant narratives are micro-level narratives whereas researcher narratives are likely to feature both observations as well as their interpretation and organisation with the means of theoretical pre-understanding. Thus, researcher narratives move us closer towards collective or macro-narratives i.e. shared views or publicly known stories that are also manifested in community and research community narratives (Elliott, 2005; Boje, 2001). For example, a community narrative on the Covid-19 pandemic in a specific country may become institutionalised into a community narrative that becomes largely shared in the particular community, i.e. country. Similarly, competing community narratives may exist regarding where and how the pandemic started. Similarly, a theoretical narrative operates at the macro-level and is shared within the theoretical paradigm (Pentland, 1999).

In terms of defining power dynamics, the narrative approach facilitates the explication of whose viewpoint is adopted, and what are the antecedents and outcomes of power dynamics and for whom. One challenge in power research may be the lack of explicit cause-outcome correlation, as the changes in power may relate to various more minor and distant events and actions. Thus, the researcher needs to have different tactics how to move from the surface description of individual elements to an understanding of how the individual elements constitute mechanisms for power dynamics. The narrative approach may facilitate this task by illuminating how the actors relevant to a given relationship and power dynamics perceive and structure the pathway of events into meaningful wholes (Pentland, 1999). This reveals potential conflicts in the details, and provides the opportunity for further data gathering or theoretical interpretation. For example, in terms of the theory, subjectivity or the sense of power are more important than the actual state or order of affairs. Similarly, the actors may differ in the degree to which they view the various elements that comprise power dynamics, which may explain the differences in description. Furthermore, such differences in description are also likely to contribute to the issue of power dynamics: the wider perspective of an actor may be the cause or outcome of the power in the relationship and power dynamics. Such analysis aims at going beyond mere description i.e. the narrative becomes a means to explain what happens to the explanation in terms of how power dynamics take place. This requires analysis of the interplay between structural and behavioural power and the purposeful and non-purposeful actions and events that drive them within and outside the focal relationship (Makkonen et al., 2012). Actions and events provide an opportunity to capture what happened and how, as they are dynamic representations of structural and behavioural power, as well as various types of actions that occur intentionally or unintentionally.

The discussion presented earlier in this chapter on power dynamics canvas is integrated into a narrative approach on power dynamics in business relationships, and is depicted in Figure 2.2. The framework focuses on an

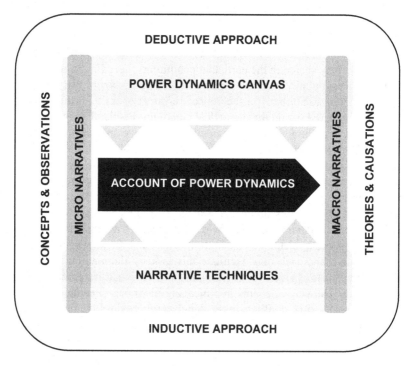

Figure 2.2 The narrative approach for power dynamics in business relationships

account of power dynamics that synthesises micro-narratives into macro-narratives with the support of the power dynamics canvas and narrative techniques. Micro-narratives refer both theoretical concepts and empirical observations, whereas macro-narratives comprise their organisation into theories and practice-oriented macro stories that articulate the causations regarding activities, events, actors, motives and context to form a unified whole. The power dynamics canvas bends towards a deductive approach, and the narrative techniques bend towards an inductive approach. The power dynamics canvas facilitates bringing in previous research in order to conceptualise power dynamics. Thus, the power dynamics canvas guides the empirical work and enables the identification of raw empirical observations as well as coding, and organises them into meaningful descriptions to ultimately be linked to existing theories. Furthermore, narrative techniques facilitate the adoption of a systematic approach for gathering the inductively emerging notions of power dynamics. Together, the elements of the framework in Figure 2.2 comprise a narrative approach on power dynamics in business relationships.

In terms of the emphasis in a given study, the logic of using different components of the framework may vary from study to study. Meanwhile, Makkonen et al. (2012) divide narrative analysis techniques into first- and second-order tactics. First-order tactics refer to using narrative analysis in accordance with other analysis techniques, whereas second-order tactics refer to interpretation and conceptual work that build towards explanatory theories for articulating the causalities. In terms of data gathering, for example, if an interview is guided by a narrative structure, an informant may reveal something relevant that would have been hidden or out of the scope of a conceptual-driven approach. Thus, the narrative approach may accommodate both deductive and inductive elements, as it is the informant who chooses the elements of the narrative, even if leading interview questions were concept-driven. In network research (Halinen & Törnroos, 2005), in particular when it comes to power dynamics that draw from various perspectives and levels of analysis, predetermining the scope may be difficult. Therefore, the narrative approach with its story structure empowers the informant to narrate not only regarding the theoretical elements asked about by the interviewee, but also regarding elements that they perceive as important for forming the story into a logical whole. Thus, the narrative structure is a kind of safety net which ensures that the relevant aspects of the phenomenon are captured. In terms of the conceptual narrative, analysis of the narrative facilitates explication of the links between the data, as well as its coding into theoretical categories and refining into conceptualisations and their relationships.

Makkonen et al. (2012) discuss several tactics regarding narrative analysis. Here we discuss further the ones that are most relevant for research on power dynamics in business relationships: *identifying and capturing key events/actors in the process, relating individual micro stories to a macro story, identifying and analysing conflicting narratives.*

The narrative analysis and power dynamics canvas are natural allies in facilitating analysis of the key events and actors in the process. The power dynamics canvas shows the interplay between power source-power target interplay, and the subjective-objective orientation that is manifested in the chain of perception, interpretation and action. Analysis of the important events is key to avoiding overly complex and relativistic analyses of potential action, reactions and re-reactions, and to distinguishing the roles of power source and power target between the actors. Narrative analysis supports event-based methodology with which Makkonen et al. (2012) develop their categorisation of contextual and focal events. Focal events represent evident actions and events that are closely linked and explicit in terms of manifesting power dynamics, whereas contextual events represent more implicit and indirect events that may happen at different levels of the context, and cast their influence over the power dynamics between the two. For example, a political conflict or natural disaster, or Covid-19 may constitute a contextual event in which different actors, industries and companies are treated unevenly, thus shaking the power structures that cause power dynamics. Narrative analysis techniques in combination with the power dynamics canvas sensitise the researcher to identifying and explicating such contextual events and analysing their role in power dynamics.

In the context of power dynamics in business relationship research, the issue of relating individual micro stories to a macro story refers to how to synthesise the buyer-supplier and power source-power target viewpoints into a relationship level account. Narrative data gathering and the narrative story structure facilitate a nuanced analysis of whether it is the power source that explicitly uses the power, or whether the power source has certain abilities that the power target values and which make the power target alter its behaviour. For example, the power source may have referent power, which is significant for the power target. In such a case, the explicit use of power by the power source is non-existent, and identifying the power requires determining how the power target perceives the effect of the power source on its behaviour. Similarly, the multifaceted nature of power dynamics in a business relationship may feature in conflicting narratives between the parties. The buyer and supplier are likely to perceive volatile events and actions from their viewpoint, and thus interpretations may differ between the parties. The narrative data structure and its thickness in contextualisation provides a means for explicating such conflicts, as well as forming a basis for further analysis. Similarly, the power dynamics canvas facilitates the explication of events and structural elements outside the focal relationship that are manifested in its power and in power dynamics.

2.1.4 Summary

The concept of power and power dynamics comprise a multi-faceted and complex subject of research. The introduced power dynamics canvas and the narrative techniques provide a basis for gathering a thick set of micronarratives and building towards macro community narratives of practice and theory. The theoretical perspectives condensed from the informants' narratives, combined with the researchers' narratives produced through balanced use of the power dynamics canvas and narrative techniques, are likely to provide a rich, multi-level theoretical account of power dynamics that is capable of shedding light on actions and events within and outside the focal relationship.

2.2 Studying relationship power dynamics – example of buyer-supplier dyads in the manufacturing industry

2.2.1 Introduction

In this chapter, the goal is to illustrate the multifaceted nature of power dynamics in business relationships with the use of interviewees' narratives or on researchers' observations. This is illustrated through the example study of interrelated components of power dynamics proposed in Figure 2.1. The illustrative study adopted a qualitative, longitudinal, multiple case research strategy to explicate the complex phenomenon of power dynamics (Yin, 2009; Piekkari et al., 2010). The longitudinal perspective provided opportunities to understand specific interrelations between buyers' and suppliers' power positions, partners' actions, and situational factors and their development over time. The four cases (Alpha, Beta, Gamma and Delta) were all chosen based on their long-term nature and the existence of substantial power asymmetry with regards to power dimensions at the beginning of these buyer-supplier relationships.

2.2.2 Multiple case study research method and research context

Multiple case study research method

In this study, we used the power bases research framework that was originally proposed by French and Raven (1959). The power base framework disaggregates power into six dimensions (see Table 1.1), which have been used in a multitude of studies (e.g. Cowan et al., 2015; Wilkinson, 1996; Siemieniako & Mitręga, 2018a; Kubacki et al., 2020). These dimensions are helpful in summing up the constituents of power at various levels regarding buyer/supplier organisations, their relationship and the operating environment of the actors (see Meehan & Wright, 2012).

Prior research has discussed the complexity of studying business network change, showing that this change may be analysed at different levels, dyads, nets and networks (Halinen et al., 1999; Möller & Halinen, 2017), and that it may be an incremental and radical change (Halinen et al., 1999). Following the agency-structure epistemological classification in social research (Giddens, 1979, 1984) and the interaction approach to understanding business networks (Ford & Håkansson, 2006; Håkansson, 1982), Makkonen et al. (2012) proposed an analytical framework where the network process is studied as an interplay between actors' agency (i.e. subjective motivations) and structure (i.e. objective forces driving actors' responses). They also suggested that their framework may be applicable to both deductive and inductive oriented studies, while in the deductive approach the structural properties of the network are identified ex ante based on a preunderstanding of the literature. Following on from their work, we have decided to treat relationship power dimensions and the positions of each business actor in these dimensions as deductively identified structural characteristics of the business relationship we investigated. Therefore, we have used "power manifestations" retrieved from our rich longitudinal data combined with literature definitions of power sources (Table 1.2) to position business actors on each investigated relationship (a)symmetry continuum. An example of how such analytical matching was conducted with regard to a particular relationship at a particular point in time, i.e. the beginning of the relationship in the Gamma case, is shown in Table 2.1. In general, we aimed to indirectly identify the power properties in the business relationships, i.e. we did not ask our informants explicitly about power using power-related notions due to the complexity and sensitivity of the topic, but instead we asked them about how the relationship with the buying (selling) company had developed, what the main challenges were and how these had been managed so far.

Apart from the structural properties of the network process, we also focused on actors' agendas, which were especially important in understanding the occurrences of power use (in contrast to the power structure), and also the extent to which power shifts could be treated as intentional. As we have focused on the evolving power properties of business dyads (Halinen et al., 1999), our analysis concentrates mostly on the mezzo level of network process (Makkonen et al., 2012), i.e. we have largely abstracted from the intra-organisational dynamics between individuals occupying various

Table 2.1 An example of the diagnostic tools used to identify buyer-supplier power positions – the start of the relationship in the Gamma case

Specification	Mediated power sources			Non-mediated power sources		
	Legitimate	*Coercive*	*Reward*	*Referent*	*Expert*	*Informational*
Power manifestations	Contractual enrolment: penalty asymmetry; range of obligations asymmetry	Conditionality in buyer's actions: moving into next cooperation stage conditioned by meeting some performance indicators	Buyer's promises i.e. shifting more of the logistics function to the supplier's side; ordering of new products next year	Buyer's world leading brand name and organisational culture admired by supplier's owners and employees	Buyer as a world leader in innovation and management acknowledged by the supplier's owners and employees	Buyer's industry leadership associated with great customer knowledge and supply chain knowledge acknowledged by the supplier's owners and employees
Information sources	Text of first contract, interview on supplier side about start of cooperation	Archival documentation of supplier's investments in facilities; archival accounting documentation; reports from buyer's audits; supplier and buyer interviewees' retrospective opinions	Archival documentation on Buyer's plans related to shifting logistics function; Supplier and buyer interviewees' retrospective insights	Secondary data accessible publicly (e.g. industry publications via Internet); Supplier and buyer interviewees' retrospective insights	Secondary data accessible publicly. Archival documentations on Buyer's management procedures and processes used by the Supplier; Interviews on Buyer's and Supplier's side	Sub-supplier's database proposed by Buyer; Buyer's regular reports on market situation (e.g. competitors and customers); Supplier interviewees' retrospective insights

Power position Substantial power asymmetry (buyer clearly has more power in all power dimensions)

positions in buying and selling companies (micro-network level), and from the dynamics of the socio-economic systems the dyads we studied were nested in (macro-network level). This approach translated into concentrating on focal events taking place at the level of business dyads understood in a similar way to Makkonen et al. (2012), i.e. time and place limited parts of network processes based on the viewpoints of key actors in the cooperating companies. As we had access to the focal events over a longer period of time, we were able to identify the evolution of power dimensions and their relations to the companies' actions. We also acknowledged the limitation of this approach as some of the focal events were most certainly leveraged by occurrences happening at other network levels. For this reason, our analysis was inclusive of such events outside the focal relationship as long as their influence was reported in the data as being associated with the power dynamics in the focal relationship. For example, we acknowledge that in the Beta case the power dynamics between buyer and seller was accelerated by governmental changes in the region, i.e. the export market. For this reason, we use the term *event* to refer to occurrences and actions that take place at any level of the context and are associated with the power dynamics of the relationships.

In our research, we followed some aspects of critical realism with regard to how to study the business relationship process (Ryan et al., 2012). Specifically, as "knowledge is always fallible and theory-laden" (idem p. 302), we have used the theory of relationship power bases originating from French and Raven (1959) to identify manifestations of the evolving power positions of actors in a business dyad. This theory was challenged in terms of the extent to which the power is "dispositional", i.e. possessed by the actor in order to have an influence over the other, while in fact a vast amount of inter-actor influences come rather from "facilitative power", which reflects norms observed among business actors and facilitated through their interactions (Hopkinson & Blois, 2014). However, we decided to use detailed power base typology as this typology is not contradictory to the dispositional/facilitative nature of power as we considered and used it, i.e. we considered that non-mediated forms of power relate to the existence of facilitative power in a business relationship. What is more, systematic focus on the evolving properties of mediated and non-mediated power in the analysed relationships allowed us to explore the interlinks between various forms of power, which was found to be important in understanding the general power amalgamate trajectory. Therefore, similarly to identifying the structural power positions, instances of using power or "power behaviour" (Oukes et al., 2019) in the dyads researched, including their consequences, were interpreted by the researchers either based on interviewees' narratives or on researchers' observations. For instance, during a regular annual business meeting, the researcher observed Buyer Beta requesting quicker realisation of orders, or Buyer Beta would be not recommending Supplier Alpha's products to new customers. The representatives of Supplier Alpha considered this suggestion to be a very serious threat to their performance on Buyer Beta's national market, and engaged in power mitigating practices as described in the research results section.

Altogether, the interview dataset comprised 49 interviews with informants, mainly senior level managers, who were involved with relationship development between their organisation and the other party over a prolonged period of time (Table 2.2). The interviews were recorded and then transcribed, coded and analysed. The average duration of the interview was 40 minutes.

Research context

The study focused on the four longitudinal buyer-supplier relationships as case studies: cases Alpha, Beta, Gamma and Delta. The cases were all studied from both sides of the dyad over different time frames (see Table 2.2). Our study looked at the general trajectories of multi-faceted power dynamics in all of the analysed cases, and therefore specific industrial features were not in the focus of our analyses. However, in this section we introduce the context that the buyers and sellers we investigated were embedded in.

Two case studies, named Alpha and Beta, concerned exchange relationships between more power full Polish company manufacturing products requiring technical expertise (Supplier Alpha) used in professional services and small foreign distributors (Buyer Alpha and Buyer Beta) with lower power position in the relationship with analysed Supplier Alpha. Delivery of these products by the manufacturer included services for distributors and professional end users (e.g. training, workshops, assistance for end user operations, designing customised products).

In the other two longitudinal business dyad case studies, named Case Gamma and Case Delta, the focus was on the outsourcing manufacturing services industry contributing value to consumer durable products. Buyer Gamma and Buyer Delta, both multinational corporation, initially had a very dominant power position with regard to various power sources in the relationships with Supplier Gamma and supplier Delta.

From the perspective of our research focus, in all four of the analysed cases the similarities dominated over the differences: there was strong power asymmetry between the business actors, and neither actor was in the position of a natural or technological monopoly. While in all the cases there were some observable relationship investments which made relationship dissolution difficult, such a radical trajectory was feasible through the

Table 2.2 Data gathering in the four longitudinal case studies

Case study code	Relationship period under investigation	Real time data gathering period	Data gathering on the supplier side	Data gathering on the buyer side
Case Alpha	(2014–2018)	(2016–2018)	*Supplier Alpha[1], 17 interviews* 1. President of Supervisory Board (2016, 2017, 2018) 2. CEO (2016) 3. Board Member (2016, 2017, 2018) 4. Sales Director (2016, 2017) 5. R&D Director (2016, 2017) 6. Export Manager (2016, 2017) 7. Senior sales specialist (2016, 2017) 8. Sales specialist (2016, 2017) Other forms of data gathering: direct observation during business meetings at supplier's location and at trade fairs; direct observations of supplier's internal sales department meetings; secondary data from emails, meeting memos , annual plans of joint buyer and supplier sales and marketing actions.	*Buyer Alpha, 2 interviews* 1. General Manager and the owner (2016, 2017) Other forms of data gathering: direct observation during business meetings at supplier's location and at trade fairs; secondary data from emails, meeting memos, annual plans of joint buyer and supplier sales and marketing actions.
Case Beta	(2012–2018)	(2016–2018)		*Buyer Beta, 2 interviews* 1. General manager and owner (2016, 2017) Other forms of data gathering: as above

Case Gamma	(1995–2018)	(2008–2018)	*Supplier Gamma, 11 interviews*	*Key customer – Buyer Gamma, 6 interviewees*
			1. CEO (2008) 2. Board Member (2010, 2016, 2017) 3. Key Account Manager (2011) 4. Business Development Director (2011, 2018) 5. Managing Director (2012) 6. Operations Director (2012) 7. Purchasing and Transport Director (2012) 8. Former CEO – Board Member (2014) Other forms of data gathering: direct observation during formal and informal meetings at supplier's and buyer's location; direct observation of supplier's internal managerial meetings; secondary data from emails, meeting memos, reports of supplier's performance, supplier's other internal documents e.g. supplier's strategic plan.	1. Senior Manager Finished Goods (2012) 2. Commodity Manager Finished Goods (2011) 3. Senior Manager, Supply Chain (2014, 2016, 2017, 2018) Other forms of data gathering: direct observation during formal and informal meeting at supplier's and buyer's location; secondary data from emails, meeting memos, buyer's reports of performance and buyer's other documents e.g. buyer's strategic plan.
Case Delta	(2004–2018)	(2004–2010, 2018)	*Supplier Delta 11 interviews* 1. Manager of Construction Office (responsible for key account management) (2004–2 interviews; 2005–1 interview; 2006–1 interview; 2007–1 interview; 2008–1 interview; 2009–1 interview; 2010–2 interviews); 2018–1 interview 2. Sales Managers, OEM services (2010) Other forms of data gathering: direct observation of interactions between representatives of the supplier and the buyer at various locations; secondary data from reports of supplier's performance, supplier's other internal documents e.g. supplier's strategic plan.	*Key customer – Buyer Delta* The information was acquired mainly through direct observation of interactions between representatives of the supplier and the buyer at various locations.

Source: Siemieniako & Mitrega, 2018b

1 Real company names concealed

availability of alternative contractors. Although we acknowledge that supply chain management (e.g. Tan, 2001) and distribution channel management (e.g. Wilkinson, 1996) may be treated as different research streams, this study generally follows a theoretical perspective, where all business relationships and business networks, either upstream or downstream, have certain similar characteristics as well as managing focal companies within such relationships (Ritter, 1999; Håkansson et al., 2009). We focused on the relationship process in the analysed buyer-supplier dyads, specifically on power asymmetry dynamics, which is possible by differentiating between the stronger and weaker sides of the business relationships.

Due to observable similarities in business relationship development and power use patterns we chose two Business-to-Business industrial settings, i.e. delivery of products requiring technical expertise for professional use, and supply of manufacturing services. Firstly, in both industries the partners were oriented rather towards long-term relationships than discrete transactions, as time was required for a satisfactory level of cooperation to be achieved. Secondly, the exit barriers in the analysed relationships in both industries were high because of the relatively high level of resources involved and the efforts needed to find a new partner. However, relationship dissolution was possible as there were alternative contractors available. Thirdly, because all the analysed suppliers were manufacturing companies and the business exchange with both OEM buyers and distributors was characterised by repeatable orders, the cooperation required systematic improvement that was more incremental over time than radical. In both these industries, radical power use was perceived as relatively risky, in comparison for instance to industries in which businesses follow a project management logic, e.g. the retail real estate development industry. In businesses governed by project logic, progress in project realisation must be done step by step, so it is not repeatable. Business partners may use power much more intensively to achieve their goals in comparison to the industries that we focused on. Fourthly, the specificity in both industries in which we analysed business dyads is such that many forms of market adaptation are necessary on the supplier's side in order to meet the buyer's particular demands. The supplier's strategy was to augment their offer by providing additional services, something that was very much expected by suppliers oriented towards customised cooperation only.

2.2.3 *Research results*

In all the case studies (Alpha, Beta, Gamma and Delta), the power position between the buyer and seller changed substantially in the long run (see Figure 2.3). In the end, in Case Alpha, the informational power advantage

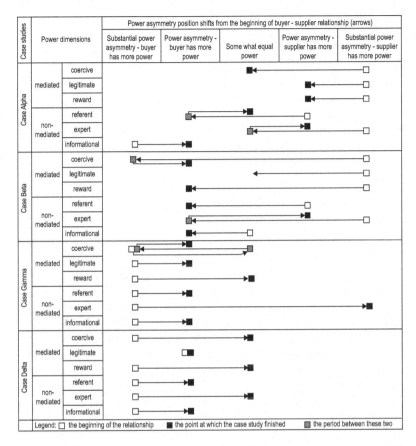

Figure 2.3 Schematic representation of power shifts in the cases being investigated

remained slightly on the buyer's side, while the power in other dimensions shifted from a clear supplier's advantage towards a relatively equal state. In terms of Case Beta, the largest shift between the beginning and end states was found in the coercive and expert power dimensions. Both of these dimensions originally built substantial power asymmetry with supplier dominance, but at the end of the investigated period, the coercive power was shifted from substantial supplier power advantage to substantial buyer power advantage. Meanwhile, expert power changed from substantial supplier power advantage to moderate supplier power advantage. The dynamics in this case relocated the other power dimensions somewhere between these extremes. In Case Gamma, all the power dimensions were initially substantially buyer dominant, whereas at the end they shifted to a buyer dominant state, except for reward power which shifted to a somewhat equal state, and expert power which shifted to a substantially supplier dominant state. In case Delta, the beginning of the relationship was very similar to case Gamma. At the end of the analysis, however, the coercive, reward and expert power dimensions shifted to a somewhat equal state, and referent and informational power shifted to a buyer dominant state. Interestingly, legitimate power did not change during the analysed period.

The next section focuses on the dynamics regarding each power dimension with reference to the analysed cases.

Mediated power

LEGITIMATE POWER

It was the general policy of Supplier Alpha to have only one representative on each domestic market. Buyers Alpha and Beta did not behave during contract negotiations in a particularly demanding way as they wanted to become the sole territorial representative of Supplier Alpha within the country. At the beginning, Supplier Alpha had an advantage in terms of the possibility to choose between Buyer Alpha or other alternative buyers on this particular market, with the same situation being observed in the case of Buyer Beta. This was a clearly identifiable example of legitimate power asymmetry, visible in the one-year contract which emphasised a clear supplier privileged position with regard to contractual provisions. This was found in both cases Alpha and Beta, in that the power shifts that occurred subsequently were similar. After the initial one-year contract had ended, the new contract between Supplier Alpha and each of these Buyers was much improved regarding coercive power. For instance, the second contract included no condition that the buyer achieve a minimum level of sales in the following 12 months, with the consequence that Supplier Alpha would be able to terminate the relationship if this level of sales was not achieved. In this case, Supplier Alpha agreed to a balanced second contract because the relationship trajectory with Buyer Alpha was exactly as expected, and there was progressive expansion into foreign markets, which a senior sales specialist at Supplier Alpha described in this way: *"They are a very good customer, cautious and loyal; not promising big expansion of our products on their local market, rather making steady growth of sales of our products by recruiting limited numbers of final user customers each year, which is constant and therefore safe for business development."* (Supplier Alpha)

The scale of relationship development in the Beta case was much greater than in the Alpha case, resulting in power shifting significantly to Buyer Beta's side, as after about four years of cooperation with Buyer Beta, the level of Supplier Alpha's sales to Buyer Beta increased rapidly by 200%, with Buyer Beta eventually accounting for 45% of the global export performance of Supplier Alpha (among 50 foreign distributors). Interestingly, an external macroenvironmental factor was identified that caused the buyer's rapid market expansion and simultaneously improved their power position in their relationship with the supplier. Specifically, this environmental factor was a change in government of a foreign country, which resulted in improvement of the buyer's position amongst end users. The impact of such an external factor on the power structure was observed on Buyer Beta's side, whose power position improved. The prolonged contract was very different in comparison to the beginning of cooperation. The cooperation with Buyer Beta was perceived by Supplier Alpha as very attractive due to the visible potential of enabling access to qualified employees. In turn, these employees were quite easy for Buyer Beta to attract in the analysed period on the country's labour market than before, in comparison to the country market of Buyer Alpha, which is an example of another exogenous factor influencing the power dynamics in the relationship with Supplier Alpha.

In the Gamma case, the dyadic relationship lasted almost 25 years and was between the powerful Buyer Gamma, a huge multinational corporation, and the medium size Supplier Gamma, offering outsourced manufacturing services for the assembly of small home appliances. The contract was much more beneficial to Buyer Gamma for many years, "We always want to have the possibility to put pressure on our suppliers" (Buyer Gamma, Senior Manager Supply Chain). Over the 15 years of cooperation, Supplier Gamma learned a lot, leveraged their expertise and expanded within the value chain, which finally allowed Supplier Gamma to negotiate a contract that was visibly better, but still with some advantage on the buyer's side.

COERCIVE POWER

We observed that coercive power was used by orchestrating manufacturers to improve cooperation efficiency and obtain other relational benefits, for instance, by requiring costly operational adjustments and investments in key competences from suppliers with the use of coercion, which was observed in the Gamma case. Another example of coercion use by a stronger supplier could be the request for information about the distributor's local market in the Alpha and Beta cases. Coercive power was also exercised by the weaker sides of the analysed relationships, when they perceived power shifts in the relationship with regard to other power dimensions to more balanced position. This was also observed in all analysed cases. More specific detailed examples are presented below based on cases Beta and Gamma.

Coercive power was exercised by Buyer Beta as a reaction to other power dimension shifts on Buyer Beta's side (see Figure 2.3). From Supplier Alpha's perspective, the relationship with Buyer Beta developed in a non-standard way in comparison to other distributors (see above in "*Legitimate power*" section), although it was very beneficial for Supplier Alpha from a financial point of view. Buyer Beta emphasised timely delivery of orders from Supplier Alpha because of the specificity of its technically complex products, which when ordered by professional end users from Buyer Beta had to be delivered quickly and on time. Buyer Beta made threats in terms of switching to different manufacturer if their conditions related to timely delivery are not met. The risk and pressure in the relationship with Buyer Beta became very problematic. Buyer Beta periodically stopped recommending Supplier Alpha's products among potential and new professional end users on their domestic market. The impact on Supplier Alpha was to make them increase the priority of timely order delivery and to ensure the development of new customised products. However, Supplier Alpha implemented countervailing power. Specifically, Supplier Alpha managed to keep the advantage with regard to their expert power, in this way becoming almost irreplaceable once more. Engaging Buyer Beta in collaborative initiatives, including current products improvement and new product development, Supplier Alpha introduced the necessity of use of new expertise, in this way increasing expert power. The expert power shift once more on to the Supplier Alpha side, which again caused more expert power on the side of the manufacturer, also impacted on decreasing the asymmetry level with regard to coercive power, from substantial power asymmetry to power asymmetry (see Figure 2.3). In practice, Supplier Alpha was more effective in managing Buyer Beta's order requests with regard to volume and time of realisation. Buyer Beta's further attempts to use coercive power were no longer so effective, as Supplier Alpha felt it was more bluffing than real threats.

In the Gamma case, the Buyer intended to keep pressure on suppliers, however Supplier Gamma achieved excellence in assembly operations and this resulted in Supplier Gamma becoming Buyer Gamma's sole OEM supplier for one type of popular product in the years 2011–2013. The supplier tried to exploit the situation and asked Buyer Gamma for better financial conditions in regular transactions, as they believed that their bargaining position had largely increased. Additionally, Supplier Gamma suggested that if this request was not fulfilled, then the cooperation would be stopped and they would take another business opportunity. Buyer Gamma considered this not to be a bluff but a realistic threat, because of the possible loss of a specific product line presence on the market until such time as assembly at another OEM supplier could be launched. Nevertheless, Buyer Gamma did not grant this request, and Supplier Gamma abandoned it, as one of the interviewees stated *"We recognized that this strategy might not work, and that they* (Buyer Gamma) *would prefer to accept the loss than agree to our conditions"* (Supplier Gamma, Board Member). Buyer Gamma reacted to the new situation and diversified purchasing, as it was not considered reasonable to have "All their eggs in one basket" (Buyer Gamma, Commodity Manager Finished Goods). Buyer Gamma ignored the increase in coercive power on Supplier Gamma's side, and when this was used, it provoked Buyer Gamma to implement supply base diversification.

REWARD POWER

Reward power was initially asymmetrical in both the Alpha and Beta cases. Supplier Alpha had the potential for positive use of power in terms of choosing Buyer Alpha and Buyer Beta as partners instead of other potential suppliers from both individual countries. The asymmetry with regard to reward power was also related to potentially rewarding Buyer Alpha and Buyer Beta for good performance according to the contract. As the relationship developed, Supplier Alpha accepted more symmetrical contract terms, but was still interested in maintaining some advantage with regard to reward source of power. One of the interviewees gave an example: "We prepared an offer for them [Buyer Alpha] and we proposed some options for the offer's conditions, with regards to prices, discounts and delivery of some free of charge services for sales support, dependent on the quantities of products ordered" (Supplier Alpha, Export Manager).

This was different in the Beta case. Due to its very strong position on the domestic market, Buyer Beta was hypothetically able to limit access for Supplier Alpha to domestic market knowledge and relationships with end user customers, which would cause strong power asymmetry with an advantage for Buyer Beta, also in terms of reward power. Such a hypothetical power shift as perceived by Supplier Alpha, would make it much easier for Buyer Beta to switch to different manufacturer, as one of the interviewees stated: "They [Buyer Beta] have such a comfortable situation on their domestic market in terms of sales stability, so despite the serious costs of switching to another supplier, I think they could do that if they wanted". (Supplier Alpha, President of Supervisory Board). Buyer Beta's increased potential for rewarding Supplier Alpha was related, for instance, to recommendation of Supplier Alpha's products among potential end users on the domestic market, conditioned on Supplier Alpha prioritising Buyer Beta's orders in manufacturing.

In the Delta case, Buyer Delta had an advantage in reward power because Supplier Delta relied very much on cross-selling. As the relationship developed, Supplier Delta also built a capacity for rewarding Buyer Delta. Supplier Delta extended the investment in inventory of components and raw materials dedicated only to Buyer Delta in order to increase its manufacturing flexibility, which meant a potential shortening for Buyer Delta of the lead time for the completion of bigger orders. Such action by Supplier Delta was conditioned on Buyer Delta fulfilling certain expectations, for instance in relation to receiving appropriate support in the implementation of new products.

Non-mediated power

EXPERT AND INFORMATIONAL POWER

We found in all the cases that substantial expert power asymmetry at the beginning of the relationship perceived by both stronger and weaker sides was an important feature, which in addition to certain other characteristics caused initiation of these analysed relationships. This was because in general the weaker sides wanted to improve their expertise capabilities, while the stronger sides were aiming at better business performance effectiveness.

In case studies Alpha and Beta, expert power was initially clearly with Supplier Alpha, which had a lot of experience, advanced technology and operational capacity in manufacturing technical products. From the perspective of Buyer Alpha and Buyer Beta, starting cooperation with Supplier Alpha meant acquiring access to quality advanced products which could be offered within their existing customer relationships at good margins and with some functionalities that the previously traded products did not have. The quality of products was largely dependent on adjustments that Supplier Alpha could make to meet the specific requirements of customers in their countries. Thus, Buyer Alpha and Buyer Beta used their informational power related to their knowledge of country-related features to make Supplier Alpha invest in their relationships and deliver customised products. Supplier Alpha conformed to this requirement and engaged in various educational activities in their relations with Buyer Alpha and Buyer Beta, e.g. "we engage a lot in increasing their expertise competences and in building their brand reliability" (Supplier Alpha. Board Member). This resulted in more knowledgeable trading partners and less Supplier Alpha dominance as an expert with regard to the products being sold. The Supplier continued investing in its distributors by conducting training for the Buyer's staff, as well as joint presentations with the Buyer's staff for local customers. This way, the Buyer learned a lot about the products that the Supplier specialised in, and at the same time became very effective in sales. However, the substantial rise of expert power on the side of the country distributors was later perceived as too great by Supplier Alpha, i.e. risky in terms of the distributors' independence. Thus, Supplier Alpha made some additional investments to leverage expert power again, which took the form of designing and providing additional services directly supporting the business processes of Buyer Alpha and Buyer Beta: *"We worked hard on delivering extra services to manifest our value support potential, e.g. through visits of our experts to this distributor's end users, developing products according to the requirements of this distributor's end users and consumers, and inviting a group of end users to a specially customized workshop."* (Supplier Alpha, Board Member)

In the Gamma case, the situation was different as the expert power shifted very much from Buyer Gamma to Supplier Gamma during cooperation, with Buyer Gamma fully accepting this direction as it leveraged Buyer Gamma's efficiency, while the Buyer did not perceive the Supplier's expertise as a risk factor because the Buyer felt that they were a clear orchestrator in the global value chain and kept dominance over Supplier Gamma in various power dimensions. Supplier Gamma fully adjusted to Buyer Gamma's technological and organisational requirements: *"we intentionally adjusted, by making an extraordinary effort, to the high demands of this customer [Buyer Gamma], because we knew we would benefit from such cooperation in the long – run, both directly in terms of development of this relationship and improving our management processes, but also indirectly through a more competitive position on the market and within the supply chain."* (Supplier Gamma, President of Supervisory Board)

Supplier Gamma used the long-term cooperation with Buyer Gamma as leverage for its own technical and organisational competence and this progress was fully acknowledged by Buyer Gamma: "In our own factory in the other country, the average time for assembling the same model of household appliance is about 40% longer than here". (Buyer Gamma, Senior Manager Finished Goods). Also "During a 'Suppliers Days Event', organized by our key customer for most important suppliers, our company was named publicly a few times as a benchmark supplier in terms of quality indicators" (Supplier Gamma, CEO). Supplier Gamma extended its operational capabilities beyond the core area of assembling small home electronic devices into the area of plastic injection molding and developing its own department for procurement of components and materials. Consequently, these changes also increased to some degree Supplier Gamma's informational power, i.e. with regard to knowledge about the value chain that Supplier Gamma and Buyer Gamma were both involved in, but this never took the form of informational dominance by Supplier Gamma.

In the Delta case, similarly to the Gamma case, inter-firm learning led to Supplier Delta's improved expert and informational power, which in turn resulted in a more balanced business relationship with a huge multinational corporation. In the first two years of cooperation, Supplier Delta was not willing to share certain information about manufacturing costs requested by Buyer Delta, as Supplier Delta was afraid of being exploited by the powerful corporation. One of the interviewees on the Supplier Delta side explained that the management board was afraid of the too strong position of Buyer Delta, which could be used against them, especially by decreasing their margin, if Buyer Delta knew the real costs of purchasing materials and components. After more or less two years of initial cooperation, when Buyer Delta did not exploit its power advantage, Supplier Delta became quite open towards information requests by Buyer Delta and started sharing information regarding costs of purchased materials and components. In turn, this information exchange resulted in more collaborative activities, including a joint project aimed at decreasing Supplier Delta's operational costs, in which the financial benefits were equally shared between the partners. The cooperation that continued after this strategic information exchange was described by Supplier's Delta representative in a very positive way.

REFERENT POWER

At the beginning of the relationship, Supplier Alpha had only a slight advantage with regards to referent power over Buyer Alpha and Buyer Beta. Buyers Alpha and Beta had a reasonable level of credibility amongst end users, as well as recognition on their domestic market. However, there was an advantage for Supplier Alpha amongst end users in terms of its internationally recognisable brand. Supplier Alpha also already had some experience on the market of Buyer Alpha and Buyer Beta. Thus, the later shift of referent power towards Buyer Alpha resulted from them merging their own image with the image of Supplier Alpha.

In the Gamma case, Buyer Gamma from the beginning had the position of being a worldwide brand, and exercised this referent power by requesting various forms of adjustments regarding e.g. management processes or technical infrastructure on the supplier side. In time, Supplier Gamma learned a lot, and as a consequence, the expert and informational power largely moved towards the supplier. This was related to a substantial increase in organisational and technical competencies, which was acknowledged not only within the dyad, but also in the whole supply chain, and resulted in acquiring new customers. These dynamics were very positively perceived by Buyer Gamma (see above with regard to expert power).

2.2.4 Summary

Discussion

The exploration of shifts in mediated and non-mediated power dimensions cross four case studies allowed to explore different drivers of power shifts in buyer-supplier relationships (see Table 2.3).

We found that power shifts were associated with intentional actions as well as more serendipitous events both within (unintentional) and outside the focal relationship – environmental and network factors. For example, macro-environmental uncertainties regarding the labour market, exchange rates of foreign currencies, the network and the value chain, all resulted in major changes and such changes in competitive positioning exercised an influence on the power capacities of the actors and respective power asymmetries in the relationships. Both weaker and stronger parties generally took variant intentional activities within the relationship as well as outside the focal relationship to reinforce their own position (Lacoste & Johnsen, 2015; Cowan et al., 2015) or to improve position of a weaker side (Siemieniako & Mitrega, 2018a), Table 2.3. While exercising power by stronger partners is in line with so far research (e.g. Buchanan, 1992; Rindt & Mouzas, 2015), we shed more light in our study on why and how weaker partners exercised power in business relationships, which is a supplement to the literature. For example in Case Gamma and Case Beta we observed that after period of successful cooperation, small partner has exercised power towards still very strong counterpart to quickly leverage financial results. However, this power exercising was treated as going beyond legitimate power use, i.e. beyond beliefs shared in the dyad (Blois, 2010) and it only motivate the partners to dynamically strengthen their own position through diversifying relationship portfolio or developing unique, not replaceable competencies.

The actors aimed at increasing their competencies to improve the offering and thus increasing the dependence of the other actor, as well as decreasing their own dependence on the other actor (Lacoste & Johnsen, 2015). Regarding the latter, for example in Case Gamma, the supplier aimed to diversify the customer portfolio to reduce the dependence and thus the power asymmetry in the relationship, whereas the buyer aimed respectively to diversify the supplier base for the same reasons (Makkonen & Olkkonen, 2013). Also, it is well visible that both, suppliers and buyers, when they were stronger parties in the relationship, initiated activities that intentionally reinforced the competencies of a weaker side which in turn influenced on partner's power capacity (see Table 2.3). Thus, our research demonstrates that in the long-run actions undertaken by partners towards each other bring indirect consequences which impact on their power position. The dominating party

Table 2.3 Specific drivers for power shifts in asymmetrical buyer-supplier relationships

	Drivers for power shifts in asymmetrical buyer-supplier relationships	Case studies names	Power dimension shifts	Power direction shifts
	Intentional actions			
Low power side	Investing in competences and specialisations required by powerful partner	Alpha, Beta, Gamma, Delta	Expert, informational	Increase of power position of a weaker side
	Making pressure on stronger partner in the next contract negotiations	Alpha, Beta,	Legitimate	
	Achieving a position of a sole supplier of concrete product	Gamma	Expert, coercive	
	Diversifying customer portfolio		Coercive, legitimate	
High power side	Keeping general policy of mediated power advantage	Gamma	Coercive, legitimate, reward	Increase of power position of a stronger side
	Diversifying suppliers base		Coercive	
	Involving weaker side into business initiatives requiring more expertise	Beta	Expert	
	Using discrete orders instead of uncomfortable contact	Delta	Coercive, legitimate	Increase of power position of a weaker side
	Sole distributor in the one country territory	Alpha, Beta	Coercive, legitimate	
	Adjustment to the weaker buyer's market development of a new products	Beta	Expert	

Unintentional actions

	Action	Companies	Power type	Result
Low power side	Rapid increase of a revenue volume	Beta, Gamma	Coercive	Increase of power position of a weaker side
	Improving market position and company image	Alpha, Beta, Gamma, Delta	Referent, expert, informational	
	Learning from the stronger party			
	Extending core capabilities beyond initial position within value chain			
High power side	Requiring costly adjustments from a weaker side to start or continue a business relationship	Gamma, Delta	Coercive	Increase of power position of a stronger side
	Investing in weaker partner's increase of competencies (e.g. sharing product-related knowledge with weaker partner)	Alpha, Beta, Gamma, Delta	Expert, informational	Increase of power position of a weaker side
	Pursuing collaborative initiatives	Beta	Coercive	
	Increased occupancy of high-power supplier's manufacturing capacity	Gamma, Delta	Expert, informational referent	
	Acknowledging supplier "excellence in operation" position among other stakeholders			

Environmental and network factors

Factor	Companies	Power type	Result
Change of the macroenvironmental factors, such us changes in government rules of particular country improve distributor's position amongst end users	Beta	Coercive, reward, referent, informational	Increase of power position of a weaker side
Change of the situation on the labour market	Alpha, Beta	Coercive	
Improvement of the conditions of making orders from sub-suppliers thanks to stronger party	Gamma, Delta	Expert, informational	
Uncertainty of exchange rates move	Gamma, Delta	Legitimate	Increase of power position of a stronger side

was putting some pressure on the subordinate for improvement of technological or sales competencies. In all analysed cases such improvements translated directly into financial benefits for the dominant, either in the form of minimising manufacturing costs or larger incomes. However, these improvements were not only relationship-specific, because the dominated companies find some ways of using these competencies elsewhere. In case of manufacturing services, we observed that suppliers being orchestrated by big brands developed their operational efficiency and management skills to the level that was not only appreciated by their partners in the dyad, but these improvements, were in time useful also beyond the dyad, i.e. in exchange with new partners. In turn, more diversified strategy in the business network meant being less dependent on the orchestrator in the value chain. In the Alpha and Beta cases involving products requiring technical expertise, the dominant's pressure to improve sales skills was evident even in the form of certain penalties written into the contract, but once the expected level of sales expertise was achieved, the weaker side formulated their own strong expectations towards initially dominating partners as they were much more confident about the value they bring to the relationship and the value that they may potentially bring to other partners. All of these demonstrates the existence of intentional as well as non-intentional shifts in power structure as well as the interconnections between non-mediated and mediated power developments in long-run relationships. We can conclude that shifts in non-mediated power influence on mediated power distribution between business partners. Considering the time periods we analysed, tensions between partners and fluctuations in relationship satisfaction, all dyads were moving towards more developed relationships, with visible increase in the value of repeated transactions, exchange being generally satisfying with regard to expected results and more cooperative efforts between partners. All of these changes signal relational exchange replacing discrete transactions (Dwyer et al., 1987). In all analysed cases the one side of relationship was initially quite clearly governing the cooperation which was visible through the contracts and the way power was used, but in time, the weaker partner has demonstrated substantial increase in the level of competencies, which made the initially dominating partner more inclined towards relationship being governed by trust. In case of technical expertise products, this increase of competencies was more visible in terms of increased turnovers on local markets, while in manufacturing services this was more visible through the operational efficiency being delivered even beyond this that was initially expected by the dominant. Taking into consideration that in all analysed cases, the multi-dimensional power was visible more symmetrical at the time we finished our observation in relation to the retrospectively analysed relationship initiation.

Our research contributes to understanding of dichotomy between "power use" and "power having" with regard to power dynamics in long-run relationships. Both of these forms seem to be meaningful and legitimate in terms of how relationships develop. The use of power as a unilateral imposition of certain unfavorable elements into the contract was clearly accepted by weaker partners in the analyzed business dyads, especially at the beginning of the cooperation, and motivated the weaker party to make extraordinary efforts to meet the contractual provisions. However, our dataset illustrates that just having some power advantage, also with regard to non-mediated power, makes an impact on the partners' behaviour. It was especially visible in manufacturing services where smaller suppliers were very motivated to invest in relationships with well-recognisable international brands as they were expecting transformative interactions, i.e. learning associated with long-run cooperation. These expectations were met in durable dyads and the expertise and image of subordinates enlarged so much that it eventually resulted in dominants accepting more partnership in terms of contract. However, our research demonstrates also some excessive forms of power use that are perceived as not legitimate by the other side and as a result, they initiate counteracting aimed at minimising further potential for such a power use. It may be treated as a form of countervailing power (see Cox et al., 2004; Lacoste & Johnsen, 2015; Siemieniako & Mitrega, 2018a; Makkonen et al., 2021), but our longitudinal research allows for interpreting it in the context of how partners prepare themselves for power dynamics. In both analysed industries, the excessive power use took the form of requesting some extra treatment and threatening if the partner does not deliver. In all of these situations, the partners not only demonstrated resistance towards such power use but also acted in a way to strengthen one's position, e.g. diversifying partners' portfolio or becoming less replaceable by contributing with more relationship-specific expertise. These actions were not resulting from general relationship development, because the relationships under consideration were very satisfactory in financial terms, however, these actions seem to result from seeing a partner going beyond consensus on the way power may be utilised and therefore signalling relationship becoming too risky. We conclude that excessive use of mediated power within business relationship accelerates power shifts.

Conclusions

The dyadic, longitudinal approach of the empirical study comprising the four cases demonstrates the analytical usefulness of the power base framework for the study of power dynamics in buyer-supplier relationships. Accordingly, the power base framework considers power asymmetry as a configuration of coercive, legitimate, reward, expert, referent and informational power dimensions. The empirical study shows that the power dimensions are a means for providing a more nuanced portrait of power asymmetry by depicting explicitly each actor's relative strength according each power dimension. Furthermore, the application of power dimensions as an analytical tool seems not to impose a choice of focus either on that between the buyer and the supplier, or that between the structural and behavioural side of power. Rather, it provides a synthesising approach (see Figure 2.1) in connecting power asymmetry to 1) the actors of buyer and supplier, and their characteristics, perceptions and interpretations, as well as 2) behavioural and structural power related actions, within and outside the focal relationships, in which the buyer and supplier engage, that manifest themselves in power dynamics.

2.3   References

Bartel, C. A., & Garud, R. (2009). The role of narratives in sustaining organizational innovation. *Organization Science*, 20(1), 107–117.

Benton, W. C., & Maloni, M. (2005). The influence of power driven buyer/seller relationships on supply chain satisfaction. *Journal of Operations Management*, 23(1), 1–22.

Blois, K. (2010). The legitimacy of power in business-to-business relationships. *Marketing Theory*, 10(2), 161–172.

Boje, D. M. (2001). *Narrative methods for organizational and communication research*. London: Sage publications.

Brown, J. R., Lusch, R. E., & Nicholson, C. Y. (1995). Power and relationship commitment: Their impact on marketing channel member performance. *Journal of Retailing*, 71(4), 363–393.

Bruner, J. (1986). *Actual minds, possible words*. Cambridge: Harvard University Press.

Buchanan, L. (1992). Vertical trade relationships: The role of dependence and symmetry in attaining organizational goals. *Journal of Marketing Research*, 29(1), 65–75.

Burrell, G., & Morgan, G. (1979). *Sociological paradigms and organizational analysis*. London: Heinemann Educational Books.

Caniëls, M. C., & Gelderman, C. J. (2007). Power and interdependence in buyer supplier relationships: A purchasing portfolio approach. *Industrial Marketing Management*, 36(2), 219–229.

Clemens, B., & Douglas, T. J. (2006). Does coercion drive firms to adopt "voluntary" green initiatives? Relationships among coercion, superior firm resources, and voluntary green initiatives. *Journal of Business Research*, 59(4), 483–491.

Cowan, K., Paswan, A. K., & Van Steenburg, E. (2015). When inter-firm relationship benefits mitigate power asymmetry. *Industrial Marketing Management*, 48, 140–148.

Cox, A., Watson, G., Lonsdale, C., & Sanderson, J. (2004). Managing appropriately in power regimes: Relationship and performance management in 12 supply chain cases. *Supply Chain Management: International Journal*, 9(5), 357–371.

Dahl, R. A. (1957). The concept of power. *Behavioral Science*, 2(3), 201–215.

Dwyer, F. R., Schurr, P. H., & Oh, S. (1987). Developing buyer-seller relationships. *Journal of Marketing*, 51(2), 11–27.

Elliott, J. (2005). *Using narrative in social research: Qualitative and quantitative approaches*. London: Sage.

Emerson, R. M. (1962). Power dependence relations. *American Sociological Review*, 27(1), 31–41.

Etgar, M. (1976). Service performance of insurance distributors. *Journal of Risk and Insurance*, 487–499.

Flick, U. (2002). *An Introduction to Qualitative Research*. London: Sage.

Ford, D., & Håkansson, H. (2006). The idea of business interaction. *IMP Journal*, 1(1), 4–27.

French, R. P., & Raven, B. (1959). The bases of social power. In D. Cartwright (Ed.), *Studies in social power* (pp. 155–164). Ann Arbor, MI: University of Michigan Press.

Giddens, A. (1979). *Central problems in social theory: Action, structure, and contradiction in social analysis*. Berkeley: University of California Press, 241.

Giddens, A. (1984). *The constitution of society: Outline of the theory of structuration*. Berkeley: University of California Press.

Habib, F., Bastl, M., & Pilbeam, C. (2015). Strategic responses to power dominance in buyer-supplier relationships: A weaker actor's perspective. *International Journal of Physical Distribution and Logistics Management*, 45(1/2), 182–203.

Håkansson, H. (1982). *International marketing and purchasing of industrial goods: An interaction approach*. IMP Project Group (Ed.). Chichester: John Wiley & Sons.

Håkansson, H., & Ford, D. (2002). How should companies interact in business networks. *Journal of Business Research*, 55(2), 133–139.

Håkansson, H., Ford, D., Gadde, L.-G., Snehota, I., & Waluszewski, A. (2009). *Business in Networks*. Chichester: John Wiley & Sons.

Halinen, A., Salmi, A., & Havila, V. (1999). From dyadic change to changing business networks: An analytical framework. *Journal of Management Studies*, 36(6), 779–794.

Halinen, A., & Törnroos, J.-Å. (2005). Using case methods in the study of contemporary business networks. *Journal of Business Research*, 58(9), 1285–1297.

Handley, S. M., & Benton, W. C. Jr. (2012). Mediated power and outsourcing relationships. *Journal of Operations Management*, 30, 253–267.

Hingley, M., Angell, R., & Campelo, A. (2015). Introduction to the special issue on power in business, customer, and market relationships. *Industrial Marketing Management*, 48, 101–102.

Hingley, M. K. (2005). Power to all our friends? Living with imbalance in supplier-retailer relationships. *Industrial Marketing Management*, 34(8), 848–858.

Hopkinson, G. C., & Blois, K. (2014). Power-base research in marketing channels: A narrative review. *International Journal of Management Review*, 6(2), 131–149.

Johnsen, R. E., Lacoste, S., & Meehan, J. (2020). Hegemony in asymmetric customer-supplier relationships. *Industrial Marketing Management*, 87, 63–75.

Kaplan, A., & Goldsen, J. M. (1965). The reliability of content analysis categories. In H. D. Lasswell (Ed.), *Language of politics* (pp. 83–112). Cambridge: MIT Press.

Krippendorff, K. (2004). *Content analysis: An introduction to its methodology*. Beverly Hills: Sage Publications.

Kubacki, K., Siemieniako, D., & Brennan, L. (2020). Building positive resilience through vulnerability analysis. *Journal of Social Marketing*, 10(4), 471–488.

Lacoste, S., & Blois, K. (2015). Suppliers' power relationships with industrial key customers. *Journal of Business and Industrial Marketing*, 30(5), 562–571.

Lacoste, S., & Johnsen, E. (2015). Supplier–customer relationships: A case study of power dynamics. *Journal of Purchasing and Supply Management*, 21, 229–240.

Makkonen, H., Aarikka-Stenroos, L., & Olkkonen, R. (2012). Narrative approach in business network process research: Implications for theory and methodology. *Industrial Marketing Management*, 41(2), 287–299.

Makkonen, H., & Olkkonen, R. (2013). The conceptual locus and functionality of key supplier management: A multi-dyadic qualitative study. *Industrial Marketing Management*, 42(2), 189–201.

Makkonen, H., & Olkkonen, R. (2017). Interactive value formation in interorganizational relationships: Dynamic interchange between value co-creation, no-creation, and co-destruction. *Marketing Theory*, 17(4), 517–535.

Makkonen, H., Siemieniako, D., & Mitręga, M. (2021). Structural and behavioural power dynamics in buyer-supplier relationships: A perceptions-based framework and a research agenda. *Technology Analysis & Strategic Management*, 1–15.

Maloni, M. J., & Benton, W. C. (2000). Power influences in the supply chain. *Journal of Business Logistics*, 21(1), 42–73.

Meehan, J., & Wright, G. H. (2011). Power priorities: A buyer–seller comparison of areas of influence. *Journal of Purchasing and Supply Management*, 17(1), 32–41.

Möller, K., & Halinen, A. (2017). Managing business and innovation networks: From strategic nets to business fields and ecosystems. *Industrial Marketing Management*, 67, 5–22.

Munksgaard, K. B., Johnsen, R. E., & Patterson, C. M. (2015). Knowing me, knowing you: Self-and collective interests in goal development in asymmetric relationships. *Industrial Marketing Management*, 48, 160–173.

Nyaga, G. N., Lynch, D. F., Marshall, D., & Ambrose, E. (2013). Power asymmetry, adaptation and collaboration in dyadic relationships involving a powerful partner. *Journal of Supply Chain Management*, 49(3), 42–65.

Ojansivu, I., Alajoutsijärvi, K., & Salo, J. (2013). The development of post-project buyer–seller interaction in service-intensive projects. *Industrial Marketing Management*, 42(8), 1318–1327.

Oukes, T., von Raesfeld, A., & Groen, A. (2019). Power in a startup's relationships with its established partners: Interactions between structural and behavioural power. *Industrial Marketing Management*, 80, 68–83.

Pentland, B. T. (1999). Building process theory with narrative: From description to explanation. *The Academy of Management Review*, 24(4), 711–724.

Pfeffer, J., & Salancik, G. R. (1978). *The external control of organizations*. New York: Harper and Row.

Piekkari, R., Plakoyiannaki, E., & Welch, C. (2010). "Good" case research in industrial marketing: Insights from research practice. *Industrial Marketing Management*, 39(1), 109–117.

Polkinghorne, D. E. (1995). Narrative configuration in qualitative analysis. In J. A. Hatch & R. Wisniewski (Eds.), *Life history and narrative* (pp. 5–24). London: Falmer Press.

Ricoeur, P. (1984). *Time and narrative*. Chicago: University of Chicago Press.

Rindt, J., & Mouzas, S. (2015). Exercising power in asymmetric relationships: The use of private rules. *Industrial Marketing Management*, 48, 202–213.

Ritchie, J., & Lewis, J. (2003). *Qualitative research practice: A guide for social science students and researchers*. London: Sage Publications.

Ritter, T. (1999). The networking company: Antecedents for coping with relationships and networks effectively. *Industrial Marketing Management*, 28(5), 467–479.

Rokkan, A., & Haughland, S. (2002). Developing relational exchange: Effectiveness and power. *European Journal of Marketing*, 36(1–2), 211–230.

Ryan, A., Tähtinen, J., Vanharanta, M., & Mainela, T. (2012). Putting critical realism to work in the study of business relationship processes. *Industrial Marketing Management*, 41(2), 300–311.

Sanderson, J. (2004). Opportunity and constraint in business-to-business relationships: Insights from strategic choice and zones of manoeuvre, *Supply Chain Management.: An International Journal*, 9(5), 392–401.

Shamsollahi, A., Chmielewski-Raimondo, D. A., Bell, S. J., & Kachouie, R. (2020). Buyer–supplier relationship dynamics: A systematic review. *Journal of the Academy of Marketing Science*, 1–19.

Siemieniako, D., & Mitręga, M. (2018a). Improving power position with regard to non-mediated power sources–the supplier's perspective. *Industrial Marketing Management*, 70, 90–100.

Siemieniako, D., & Mitręga, M. (2018b). *Is it good to balance power in a buyer-seller "business marriage" and how it happens?* 34th IMP Conference: From Business to Research and Back Again, Kedge Business School, Marseille Campus, Marseille, France 4–7.09.2018. Available at: www.impgroup.org/paper_view.php?viewPaper=9889 [data of access: 2021.11.12].

Tan, K. C. (2001). A framework of supply chain management literature. *European Journal of Purchasing Supply Management*, 7(1), 39–48.

Ulrich, D., & Barney, J. B. (1984). Perspectives in organizations: Resource dependence, efficiency, and population. *Academy of Management Review*, 9(3), 471–481.

Wilkinson, I. F. (1996). Distribution channel management: Power considerations. *International Journal of Physical Distribution & Logistics Management*, 26(5), 31–42.

Wilson, D. F. (2000). Why divide consumer and organizational buyer behaviour? *European Journal of Marketing*, 34(7), 780–796.

Wolfe, R. J., & McGinn, K. L. (2005). Perceived relative power and its influence on negotiations. *Group Decision and Negotiation*, 14(1), 3–20.

Xuan, P. A. N., Shuwei, Z. A. N. G., Yiyang, H. U., & Jinyang, L. I. U. (2020). Identifying the positive sides of power use between (in) congruence in distributive fairness perception and supplier-buyer relationship quality. *Industrial Marketing Management*, 91, 362–372.

Yin, R. K. (2009). *Case study research: Design and methods*. 4th ed. Thousand Oaks: Sage Publications, Inc.

Zadykowicz, A., Chmielewski, K., & Siemieniako, D. (2020). Proactive customer orientation and joint learning capabilities in collaborative machine to machine innovation technology development: The case study of automotive equipment manufacturer. *Oeconomia Copernicana*, 11(3), 415–423.

Zhao, X., Huo, B., Flynn, B. B., & Yeung, J. H. Y. (2008). The impact of power and relationship commitment on the integration between manufacturers and customers in a supply chain. *Journal of Operations Management*, 26(3), 368–388.

3 Power in international business relationships

3.1 The specific nature of power in international business relationships

3.1.1 Introduction

This chapter provides an insight into the special nature of power in international business relations. First, we consider power in light of the characteristics of a dynamic and turbulent international business environment. We argue that power is a reflection of dependence, with contrasting phenomena on the same continuum, although clearly supporting the position that limited dependence leads to low power due to low attention to the relationship. Although the most common response of the weaker party in an asymmetric, imbalanced dependency is no response, the weaker party may fight back by using one of the following types of counterstrategies (Coughlan et al., 2006): (1) developing alternatives (e.g. diversifying the product portfolio, offering greater benefits, making oneself more unusual, etc.), (2) organising a coalition to attack the partner's power (e.g. lobbying, using third parties, arbitration to settle disputes, etc.), (3) terminating the relationship as the most drastic action. We extend this view from the literature on international marketing channels by considering a typical asymmetric business relationship that we observe in the literature on headquarters-subsidiary relationships. The main contribution of this chapter is to bring the two theoretical streams together by examining power in asymmetric international relationships.

3.1.2 The role of power in international business relationships

International business relationships arise under the special conditions of a volatile, complex, dynamically changing and evolving international business environment, in which a large degree of geographical and cultural

DOI: 10.4324/9781003095934-4

separation between exporters and importers, as well as the existence of dissimilarities in business mentality, risk assessment, politico-legal systems and languages, make it difficult to deepen international business relationships (Katsikeas & Piercy, 1992). These features of international business relationships contribute to an exacerbation of potential conflicts, an alteration of the flow of information between interacting parties and communication failures (Leonidou et al., 2019), suggesting that the role of power in the international environment may be quite different from that in the domestic one. There are even studies (e.g. Johnson et al., 1993) that show that the mediated and non-mediated bases of power found in domestic relationships were not replicated in the perceptions of foreign distributors.

Following the most commonly cited definition of power in international marketing literature, in which power is defined as "the ability of one member of the marketing channel to control the decision variables in the marketing strategy of another member in a particular channel at a different level of distribution" (El-Ansary & Stern, 1972), power in international business relationships refers to the exporter's ability to get an overseas importer to do something it would not otherwise have done (Kaleka et al., 1997). Overseas importers have access to information about market conditions and the end consumer, so they are able to exert power over suppliers who have limited resources for establishing marketing channels with similar economic advantages (Matanda & Freeman, 2009). On the importers' side, they have been found to exercise mediated power (see section 1.1 for an explanation) in rare to moderate cases, with reward and coercive power being used more frequently, while non-mediated power is used relatively frequently, and expert power (e.g. their knowledge of foreign markets) most frequently (Leonidou & Katsikeas, 2003). However, when the relationship is characterised by asymmetric power, the more powerful party is more likely to use coercive power than non-coercive power to impact the behaviour of the less powerful member of the international distribution channel (Matanda & Freeman, 2009).

Power is present in virtually all elements of international distribution channels as they consist of mutually interdependent actors, with interdependence being managed through the use of power (Coughlan et al., 2006). The literature (e.g. Gaski, 1984) argues that global buyers could extract asymmetrically higher value than their production suppliers because of their exclusive access to end customers (Pham & Petersen, 2021):

> The market or channel power of global buyers is based on a combination of strong brands, anticipated distribution channels, and private information about end users. The leading firm, often a global buyer, receives the "lion's share" in return for its proprietary designs, technologies, brands, or pre-emptive market access.

Using the criterion of the nature and intensity of importers' power, Leonidou and Katsikeas (2003) identified four types of exporting firms. Inert Complacents (low non-mediated power, low mediated power) are exporters who have a lot of trust in and dependence on the relationship, but at the same time have little connection to importers due to limited communication, loose cooperation and coordination, and infrequent social contact. As a result, their inertness leads to negative financial performance. Problematic Satisfiers (low non-mediated power, high mediated power) are exporters that are highly dependent on their importers, who exercise high levels of mediated power. Their relationship is characterised by low trust and understanding, mild conflicts and high collective performance. Collaborative Strugglers (high non-mediated power, low mediated power) are exporters who enjoy relatively high trust, strong commitment, strong cooperation and communication, very low conflict, low dependence and high satisfaction with the behavioural outcomes from their relationship with importers. Hazardous Agitators (high non-mediated power, high mediated power) are exporters who face high levels of power exercised by importers, leading to distrust, distance and uncertainty in their relationship. Such exporter-importer relationships are doomed to stagnate or dissolve due to low levels of both financial and behavioural satisfaction. Overall, the results show that the combination of a high level of power and a low level of power leads to much greater satisfaction than the other two extremes.

Antecedents to power in international business relationships

HOST COUNTRY DEVELOPMENT

Exporters based in developing countries are under the influence of a higher degree of power exercised by importers from developed countries because of the latter's greater control over international marketing decisions (Katsikeas & Piercy, 1992). Therefore, for exporters to exercise their power, it is imperative that they develop international marketing capabilities that will enable them to become familiar with the forces that influence their export markets. In this context, it is the responsibility of importers from developed countries to take a proactive role in creating an equal partnership with exporters from countries with lower levels of development.

INSTITUTIONAL FACTORS

Institutional factors in international markets (e.g. perceived market foreignness, environmental uncertainty, regulatory volatility) contribute to higher levels of exercised power (Matanda & Freeman, 2009; Leonidou et al., 2019). In particular, the coercive power of foreign buyers leads exporting manufacturers to cooperate in circumstances of perceived high competitive intensity and high market turbulence (Matanda & Freeman, 2009).

Parties that are heavily involved in international business relationships (i.e. regular exporters, compared to firms with sporadic export involvement) tend to exercise more power over sales and promotional strategies, confirming that the degree of power exercised may vary depending on the international involvement of the business partner (Kaleka et al., 1997). In other words, the mode chosen for entering the foreign market determines the degree of power exercised. On the one hand, exporters that choose one mode of export entry (e.g. agents, distributors, export buying agent) have little control over international operations and thus less power in international business relationships. On the other hand, firms that choose to invest more heavily in foreign operations (e.g. franchising, joint ventures, mergers and acquisitions, wholly owned subsidiaries) have greater control over foreign operations and exercise a higher degree of power. Similarly, international exposure can be interpreted through the degree to which the international marketing strategy is adapted to the foreign market. Firms that adapt their international marketing strategy (e.g. price, promotion, distribution) have stronger bargaining power in foreign business relationships than firms that do not adapt their strategies at all. In addition, international companies that adapt their products to local needs or create a brand to address local characteristics have a higher degree of power compared to companies that only adapt other parts of the international marketing strategy.

CULTURE

The reactions of the parties involved in a business relationship to the power exercised have been found to vary by culture (Johnson et al., 1993). The authors studied US-Japanese business relationships and found that their negotiation process is very different (e.g. Japanese teams differ in the size and structure of their negotiating teams, and require and use significantly more information and time in the process than American teams). Their research confirmed that the Japanese appear to view power in a paternalistic context (i.e. the use of power as authoritative or facilitative) rather than in the dichotomy of mediated and non-mediated power found in US research or in Western cultures, which may contribute to the prevalence of paternalistic vertical relationships in Japanese culture and business. These findings are of great importance to practitioners, as their traditional use of power toward Japanese people may be misinterpreted and misperceived by their Japanese business partners (e.g. US managers who attempt to make their voices heard through an aggressive form of power use may be viewed as out of line and not taken seriously by their Japanese business partners; on the other hand, the Japanese may feel that their business partners are more committed to the relationship because they care enough to manage and lead them).

POWER SOURCES THEMSELVES
Finally, the sources of power of foreign distributors are interrelated in their relationship with export manufacturers. It was found that foreign distributors' use of reward power is positively related to export producers' perceived expert, legitimate, referent and informational sources of power. In addition, importers' use of coercive power is negatively related to informational power over exporters (Katsikeas et al., 2000). For an overview of the antecedents to power in the international context, see Figure 3.1.

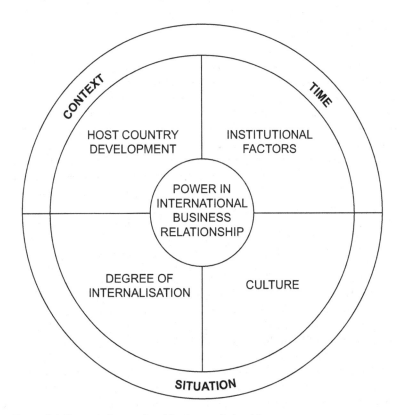

Figure 3.1 Power in international business relationships

Outcomes of power in international business relationships

Higher levels of coercive power exercised by the exporter in exporter-importer relations lead to higher levels of distance, opportunism and uncertainty (Leonidou et al., 2019). As the exercise of coercive power leads to misunderstanding, tension and frustration (Leonidou et al., 2008), the exercise of coercive power by one party will increase the psychic or cultural distance from the other party (Leonidou et al., 2019). Significant psychological and geographical distance between exporters and importers, the difficulties in controlling a foreign business partner's business conduct, and the high costs associated with coordination and communication with the international business partner contribute to increased opportunistic behaviour (Leonidou et al., 2019). Moreover, the exercise of coercive power leads to turbulence in the exporter-importer relationship, which in turn increases uncertainty in the relationship (Leonidou et al., 2008), which is associated with doubts about the business partner's intentions, ambiguity about the relationship behaviour and information asymmetry between the parties, which makes it difficult to evaluate the relationship in terms of costs and benefits (Leonidou et al., 2019).

Higher levels of non-coercive power (i.e. reward, expert, legitimating and referent power) exercised by the exporter in the exporter-importer relationship lead in turn to lower levels of distance, opportunism and uncertainty (Leonidou et al., 2019). The exporter's use of non-coercive sources of power to influence the importer creates a favourable climate in the relationship (Leonidou et al., 2019) characterised by less conflict (Leonidou et al., 2008), better understanding (Leonidou & Katsikeas, 2003) and greater trust (Jain et al., 2014). As the relationship characterised by the power exercised by the exporter without coercion is reciprocal, both parties are encouraged to work towards common goals rather than pursuing their own interests (Nyaga et al., 2013), to be more open and trustworthy in communication, and to use a problem-solving approach to conflict resolution, thus reducing the possibility of opportunism (Leonidou et al., 2019). Indeed, the use of non-coercive power by the exporter motivates the importer to be more accommodating in the relationship by providing more value in the form of knowledge or relationship-specific investments (Nyaga et al., 2013). Consequently, non-coercive power facilitates higher levels of coordination and cooperation, creating a state of calm in the relationship and reducing uncertainty (Leonidou et al., 2019).

US exporter satisfaction with Southeast Asian importers was found to be positively and significantly correlated with noncoercive power, unexercised power, trust and dependence, but negatively correlated with coercive power (Raven et al., 1993). Non-coercive sources of power are a better alternative than coercive sources of power for improving the satisfaction of weak international distribution channel members (Hunt & Nevin, 1974). Considering dependence as a phenomenon opposite to power, research has found that when there is dependence asymmetry between business partners, a Chinese firm is more likely to pursue legitimacy through external legitimacy measures, while a Western firm is more likely to look for legitimacy through internal legitimacy measures (Zeng et al., 2020).

Since perceived service quality is an element of a differentiation strategy and used as a critical determinant in supplier evaluation and purchasing decisions in the dyad between the manufacturer and the foreign distributor, the service quality of the international distribution channel can be regarded as a kind of power used to influence and control distributors' decisions and behaviours. International distribution channels require greater effort and financial risk for manufacturers because they have less control over service levels due to diversity in channel levels, long shipping distances, numerous international shipments and different time zones (de Ruyter et al., 1996). The existing literature provides ambiguous results. On the one hand, in the case of a franchisor-franchisee relationship, perceived power decreases when the quality of products and services increases (Hunt & Nevin, 1974), which the authors themselves argue is unreasonable and makes the observed relationships appear spurious. On the other hand, perceived service quality is considered an example of non-coercive power, and as such has been found to be positively related to and a relatively more an element of perceived relationship strength than coercive power (de Ruyter et al., 1996).

3.1.3   Power in headquarters-subsidiary relationships

Similar to international marketing channels, subsidiaries are also organised through reciprocal exchanges (Birkinshaw et al., 2000). Therefore, the study of headquarters-subsidiary relationships remains crucial for understanding MNCs as inter-organisational networks and their relational atmospheric characteristics such as power. Power in the relationship between headquarters and a subsidiary reflects the hierarchical nature of such relationships (Kostova et al., 2016). Interdependence and an imbalance of dependencies explain the power of subsidiaries (Mudambi et al., 2014). Functional power, through the possession of technological power rather than business power, or the possession of both, enhances the strategic power of the subsidiary in the MNC network (Mudambi et al., 2014).

In the earlier stages of subsidiary development, the relationships between headquarters and subsidiaries are governed by agency theory (i.e. the notion that subsidiary managers must be controlled by headquarters), and subsidiary decision rights are "borrowed" from the headquarters. In the later stages, resource dependency theory and the notion that subsidiary managers can develop their own path apply (Cuervo-Cazurra et al., 2019). See Figure 3.2 for an illustration of the relationship between power and relationship status in light of the above theories.

Headquarters and subsidiary managers differ in their perception of the subsidiary's role in the MNC (Birkinshaw et al., 2000). While headquarters strives to maintain control over the headquarters-subsidiary relationship to ensure efficiency and strategic direction throughout the MNC, subsidiaries seek greater autonomy (Ambos et al., 2011). These different tendencies have important implications for the management of headquarters-subsidiary relationships (Birkinshaw et al., 2000).

Headquarters-subsidiary relations in MNCs can be conceptualised as a multi-level discursive struggle between key managers (Koveshnikov et al., 2017): at the 1st level – a discursive struggle for actions and decisions using a rationalist approach; at the 2nd level – a discursive struggle for power relations using autonomy and control; and at the 3rd level – a discursive struggle for power relations using autonomy and control.

The power of subsidiaries differs according to their position in the value chain of the MNC network (i.e. producing vs. downstream subsidiaries). Moreover, the pattern of power distribution in the MNC network creates a unique structural feature of the power structure in MNCs, ranging from an oligopolistic structure (a small number of subsidiaries possess concentrated power) to an egalitarian structure (evenly distributed power in all subsidiaries). The structural characteristics of a range of subsidiaries in the MNC network are vital factors affecting power in the headquarters-subsidiary relationship, relationship management and MNC performance (Lee, 2021). The headquarters-subsidiary relationship is embedded in a dynamic international environment and consequently evolves dynamically, resulting in power positions changing over time (Ambos et al., 2011).

Subsidiaries can gain more power and autonomy by building trust and networking with the headquarters (Ambos et al., 2011). When subsidiary managers overestimate their role, the headquarters exerts greater control over the subsidiary, which in turn is associated with lower levels of cooperation in their relationship (Birkinshaw et al., 2000). The power of the headquarters is based on its formal authority to control critical resources and be the sole provider of corporation-wide shaping strategy (Yamin & Forsgren, 2006).

Reverse knowledge transfer, i.e. the transfer of knowledge from the subsidiary to the headquarters (e.g. market and marketing data, sales, research), has a positive impact on the subsidiary's power and its autonomy to exert influence over the headquarters (Najafi-Tavani et al., 2015). This finding is consistent with previous research on the reinforcing power of partners on the receiving end of asymmetric relationships, and the role of soft power in asymmetric relationships (Hingley et al., 2015).

Embeddedness in host country networks can possibly be considered a cause of power for affiliates, as they can use knowledge-based resources (information power) rooted in their relationships with external partners to influence headquarters, which has no control over these resources. Subsidiary embeddedness is defined as "mutual adjustments in the development of processes and products between a focal subsidiary and a small number of host partners (customers, suppliers, research centres and universities) with which the subsidiary has established enduring business relationships" (Yamin & Forsgren, 2006). As such, embeddedness is considered as the strategic power of the subsidiary and is different from other sources of power that arise from the subsidiary's position in interpreting the local environment. It has been found that the relative power of the subsidiary within a larger MNC is stronger when the degree of internal embeddedness is high, and weaker when the degree of external embeddedness is high (Najafi-Tavani et al., 2015).

The interests and perceptions of the headquarters and the subsidiary often do not align (i.e. a dyadic relationship with mixed motives or a perception gap), usually due to the subsidiary's desire for autonomy versus the headquarters' desire for control, the subsidiary's entrepreneurial aspirations versus the headquarters' perception of opportunism, and the interests of the local environment versus global profitability (Ghoshal & Noria, 1989).

The literature distinguishes four real types of subsidiary power (Dörrenbächer & Gammelgaard, 2011): systemic, resource, institutional and micropolitical. Systemic power refers to the subsidiary's specialisation in a particular function or value-adding activity (e.g. production, sales, design, etc.) in the firm's internal division of labour, which is critical to the proper functioning of the MNC's value chain. Resource dependence power is the most frequently cited source of subsidiary power and appears to be the most enduring and powerful among the four powers mentioned, as the subsidiary has control over critical resources such as market knowledge, market access, or membership in an innovative business network that may be critical to the performance of the MNC as a whole. Institutional power refers to the host country's institutional structures (e.g. laws and regulations, norms and values) that are reflected in the subsidiary's power. Micropolitical bargaining power is explained by "situations in which subsidiaries exert their influence on headquarters through a combination of their own initiatives, manipulative behaviour, strategic information policy and issue selling" (Dörrenbächer & Gammelgaard, 2011).

On the one hand, to get approval for implementation of subsidiary initiatives in less asymmetric power relationships between headquarters and

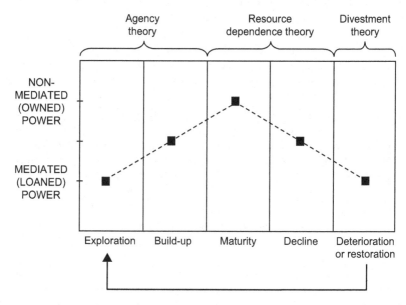

Figure 3.2 Power and international relationship status

Source: Based on Jap & Ganesan, 2000; Cuervo-Cazurra et al., 2019; Leonidou et al., 2019.

subsidiaries (i.e. subsidiaries are fairly powerful in these relationships), a low level of issue selling is required. On the other hand, highly asymmetric relationships suggest a high necessity for issue selling, which is rarely enough to obtain headquarters' approval. Consequently, issue selling can be understood as a secondary power in subsidiary initiatives, as it only works in combination with the power of the subsidiary (Dörrenbächer & Gammelgaard, 2016).

Bartlett and Ghoshal (1986) propose a framework for greater differentiation in the strategic roles assigned to different subsidiaries. Based on the criteria of the strategic importance of the regional environment and the subsidiary's capabilities, the authors distinguish between four strategic roles of subsidiaries (see Figure 3.3): implementer, black hole, contributor and strategic leader. Strategic leaders are subsidiaries that have the strongest relationship with headquarters and collaborate with it in developing and implementing strategy. In this case, the subsidiary is a "sensor of signals of change" in analysing international threats and opportunities, and therefore is often responsible for developing appropriate responses to dynamic changes in the global environment. Subsidiaries that similarly to strategic leaders

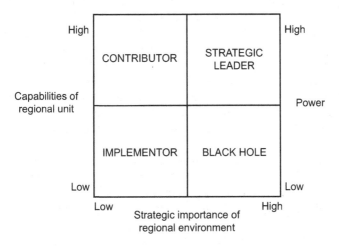

Figure 3.3 Strategic roles of subsidiaries and power in their relationship with head-quarters

Source: Adapted from Bartlett & Ghoshal, 1986.

have a high level of specific capabilities (i.e. contributors) tend to operate in smaller markets. Typically, these subsidiaries have competitive advantages in R&D, creativity, design and sometimes production; therefore, they are usually considered centres of excellence. Such subsidiaries can be important laboratories for implementing new ideas and testing change in large multinationals, and are quite typical in small highly-developed countries. An implementer subsidiary operates in a less strategically important market and has just enough capacity to maintain its local market presence. This is reflected in limited market potential and resource allocation. This is the most typical role of an MNC's subsidiary, usually located in developing or lesser-developed countries, where subsidiaries are seen as suppliers of the MNC's value added. They usually have the important role of laying the foundations for the MNC's expansion, and provide strategic leverage for the MNC. Black holes are subsidiaries in markets with a strong local presence and competition, whose objective is not to "manage the hole" but to find a way out. These subsidiaries face the challenge of establishing a significant market presence in a large, demanding and competitive national environment, which has proven to be extremely difficult, time-consuming and expensive. Black holes are usually reorganised as "sensory outposts" whose role is to learn new technologies, and monitor the market, trends and R&D of other companies on the market, as well as create a learning base for the MNC.

We contribute to this framework by suggesting that in a situation where a subsidiary's capabilities and the strategic importance of the regional environment are high, the subsidiary's power will also be high, and vice versa. Consequently, strategic leaders will be able to exert a higher degree of power over headquarters than implementers on the other side of the power spectrum. Black holes will most likely not be able to exercise power in their relationship with headquarters due to their limited resources and capabilities. Contributors, although operating in a less strategic market, contribute significantly to the overall performance of the MNC, so their power will also be high.

The nature of corporate control as a consequence of the power exercised in the head office-subsidiary relationship may differ systematically from subsidiary to subsidiary. In light of this, Gupta and Govindarajan (1991) analyse the dissimilarities in the strategic context of subsidiaries in two aspects: a) the extent to which the subsidiary is a user of knowledge from the rest of the MNC (i.e. transfer of expertise such as purchasing, product, design or marketing skills, and/or external market data of strategic value such as information about suppliers, customers and competitors), and b) the extent to which the subsidiary is a provider of such knowledge to the rest of the MNC. Based on these two dimensions, the authors propose four roles for subsidiaries (see Figure 3.4): global innovator, integrated player, implementor and local innovator. A global innovator is a subsidiary that is characterised as the "source" of knowledge for other entities, and is usually historically the domestic entity. An integrated player creates knowledge for others in a similar way to a global innovator, but unlike the global innovator is not self-sufficient in its own knowledge needs. Implementors are

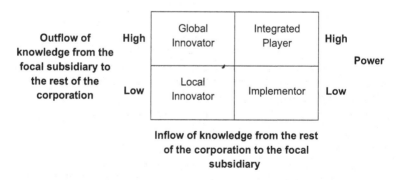

Figure 3.4 The relationship between power and knowledge transfer between headquarters and subsidiaries

Source: Adapted from Gupta & Govindarajan, 1991.

subsidiaries that create little knowledge of their own and rely heavily on incoming knowledge from headquarters or other subsidiaries. A local innovator is a subsidiary that is almost entirely responsible locally for creating relevant knowledge in all business areas and functions, while its knowledge is considered too specific to be of use to others.

We contribute to this framework by suggesting the possibility that the power exercised is higher for global innovators and integrated actors than for local innovators and implementers. The reasons for this lie in the sources of affiliate power shown in Figure 3.5. As can be seen from the figure, global innovators and integrated players exhibit moderate to high levels of lateral independence, a need for autonomous initiative and levels of global authority. Implementors and local innovators exhibit low to medium levels of lateral interdependence, a need for autonomous initiative and levels of global authority, so their power is lower. In summary, knowledge flow within an MNC is considered one of the most important determinants of subsidiary power (Mudambi & Navarre, 2004). A subsidiary's perceived power influence on interpersonal knowledge transfer within the MNC can be explained through cultural intelligence and identification with the organisation, as

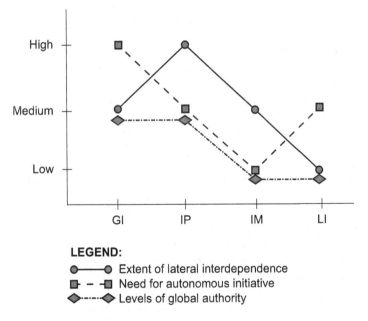

LEGEND:
● —— ● Extent of lateral interdependence
■ – – ■ Need for autonomous initiative
◆ ---- ◆ Levels of global authority

Figure 3.5 Subsidiary strategic context and sources of subsidiary power

GI = Global Innovator, IP = Integrated Player, IM= Implementor, LI = Local Innovator
Source: Adapted from Gupta & Govindarajan, 1991.

shown by Phookan and Sharma (2021). Their study confirms that perceived subsidiary power contributes positively and directly to knowledge sharing, and indirectly to knowledge seeking through identification with the organisation. Moreover, cultural intelligence acts as a moderator of the indirect effect of a subsidiary's perceived power on the search for knowledge.

Subsidiary power can also be assessed in terms of two key dimensions of headquarters-subsidiary relationship dynamics, which Bouquet and Birkinshaw (2008) have termed weight and voice. These are used by subsidiaries to attract the attention of headquarters, while headquarters has a natural tendency toward standardisation and control. These two dimensions were developed in response to the importance of headquarters being attentive to important subsidiaries (Bartlett & Ghoshal, 1986), and the importance of subsidiaries attracting attention and expressing their achievements (Birkinshaw et al., 2000). Weight is related to the structural position within the network that attracts the attention of the headquarters, while voice refers to the relationship process in which the subsidiary highlights its existing or potential contribution to the MNC. Subsidiary weight (also referred to as the structural determinant of subsidiary attention) refers to the strategic importance of the local market (i.e. the perceived critical importance of the particular market in which a subsidiary operates to the overall performance of the MNC), and the strength of the subsidiary within the MNC network (i.e. the extent to which the subsidiary performs activities on which other subsidiaries in the MNC network depend). Subsidiary voice (also referred to as the relational determinant of subsidiary attention) refers to the taking of initiatives (i.e. deliberate and intentional voluntary actions by subsidiary managers aimed at enhancing the subsidiary's perceived importance and status in the MNC network and focused on new products and opportunities), and profile building (i.e. actions taken by subsidiary managers to enhance their reputation, credibility and image). Considering the weight and voice of the subsidiary (see Figure 3.6), we assume that subsidiaries with high weight and voice have a higher level of power than subsidiaries with low voice and weight, while a high level of only one of the two dimensions would guarantee a subsidiary a medium level of power.

Positive attention by headquarters, defined as "the extent to which a parent company recognises and appreciates a subsidiary for its contribution to the MNE as a whole" (Bouquet & Birkinshaw, 2008), consists of three subconstructs: a) relative attention (i.e. the perceived level of recognition and appreciation given by headquarters to a focal subsidiary compared to other subsidiaries in the MNC), which is both a scarce commodity and a competitive process that depends on geographic distance and downstream competence; b) supportive attention (i.e. HQ's provision of resources, such as best practices, technology, people and career opportunities, to support subsidiary

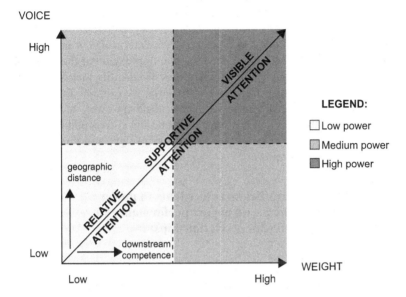

Figure 3.6 Power and subsidiary weight and voice

Source: Based on Birkinshaw et al. (2000) and Bouquet & Birkinshaw (2008).

development) as a type of "emotional energy" that describes HQ's value-adding interventions; and c) visible attention (i.e. HQ's explicit recognition of subsidiary performance in corporate communications with various stakeholders), which gives subsidiaries the highest voice and weight. It was found that formal attention from headquarters fully mediates the relationship between reverse innovation transfer and subsidiary power, while the relationship is moderated by the specificity of corporate culture and the intensity of intra-firm competition (Wang et al., 2019).

3.1.4 Summary

This chapter provides a unique comparison between the literature on international marketing channels and the literature on headquarters-subsidiary relations. We first address the specifics of power in international business relationships. We identify four factors specific to international business relationships (culture, institutional factors, host country development, degree of internationalisation) that constitute power in international business relationships. We assume that international business relationships evolve dynamically, and theorise why mediated power is more often exercised at the beginning and end of the relationship cycle and non-mediated power at the peak of the business relationship. We examine power in headquarters-subsidiary relationships from several perspectives. First, considering the strategic importance of the regional environment and the subsidiary's capabilities, we identify four subsidiary roles and their corresponding power. Similarly, we examine the inflows and outflows of knowledge transfer at the subsidiary level, and identify four types of innovators in the subsidiary and the corresponding power they wield. Finally, we bring the concepts of weight and voice to the analysis of subsidiary power.

3.2   Culture and conflict as antecedents to power and their influence on export performance in international business relationships[1]

3.2.1   *Introduction*

This chapter addresses the most commonly studied antecedents to power and their consequences for export performance in international business relationships. The relationship between power, conflict and performance has been widely studied in the areas of international marketing channels, headquarters-subsidiary relationships, negotiation behaviours and strategies, conflict resolution, sociology and psychology. Despite the considerable attention given to the phenomenon in the extant literature, the findings are inconclusive and require primarily interdisciplinary studies. This chapter provides an up-to-date overview of the phenomenon and the relationships that have been explored in the existing literature. When we look at the phenomenon from the perspective of international business relationships, it is absolutely crucial for at least two reasons to first examine the role of culture. First, culture can help us better understand the relationships between power and other phenomena. For example, a study of international business relationships between the United States and Mexico found that business partners' sensitivity to national business culture reduces conflict and improves communication, both of which lead to better export performance (LaBahn & Harich, 1997). Second, we assume that the international business environment is dynamically changing, and so is the culture that needs to be interpreted in any particular context. For example, the causes of conflict may be culture-specific. What is considered coercive power in one culture and leads to conflict, is seen as respect for norms and legitimate power in another culture (Coughlan et al., 2006; Zhou et al., 2007).

3.2.2 Culture and power in international business relationships

"The decision to project power is itself a culturally constituted act, as are the forms and reasons for its projection" (Black & Avruch, 1993, p. 385). Differences in perceived projection and reception can be attributed to cultural differences. Many of the serious difficulties encountered in international relationships can be attributed to what is known as "cultural blindness", which refers to the failure of business partners to perceive the profound differences in meaning that each party attributes to important features of the relationship. Cultural blindness is often due to unconscious predispositions and ethnocentrism, particularly the ethnocentrism of those in power. Mutually desired goals and lasting international relationships can only be achieved if there is an awareness of cultural differences.

To some extent, "inter-firm relations have been recognised as a driving force of internationalization" (Axelsson & Agndal, 2000). Researchers in international business have found that

> establishing, developing and maintaining successful business relationships with distant partners is not an easy task, . . . due to the major barrier in the form of cultural distance, . . . while ethnocentrism negatively affects cultural sensitivity and the quality of relationships between exporters and importers.
>
> (Trang et al., 2003)

Cultural distance has a negative impact on the power of individuals and positions, affecting the combination of person and exploration more than the combination of position and exploitation (Malik & Yazar, 2016). Asymmetric power between individuals leads to asymmetric social distance, where individuals with high power feel more distanced than individuals with low power (Magee & Smith, 2013). Drogendijk and Holm (2012) examined the effect of culture on headquarters-subsidiary relationships and found that

> low cultural distance relationships differ significantly in terms of headquarters influence depending on whether headquarters and subsidiary agree to accept or reject power differentials . . . and similarly, high cultural distance relationships differ according to whether the headquarters or subsidiary is from a high power distance culture.

Their study confirms that a subsidiary's acceptance of power differentials influences the headquarters' level of influence.

From a cultural perspective, power increases the extent to which individuals experience authenticity. Power has been found to decrease happiness in a collectivist society, as authenticity is a less important predictor of happiness in a collectivist culture (Datu & Reyes, 2015). In examining the cultural impact on relationships, empirical research has confirmed that stereotypes are present in the early stages of a relationship and may hinder the later progress of a potential partnership (Carr, 2002). Moreover, the behaviour of low-power business partners is influenced by their culture and the culture of the high-power counterparty. For example, a Hong Kong manager with low power in a collectivist hierarchical culture that emphasises group alignment and power differentials, adapted his behaviour and level of cooperation to the foreign manager with high power with whom he interacted (Kopelman et al., 2016). Finally, the exercise of power in Western cultures has been found to be based on rationality and bureaucracy, whereas in Eastern cultures it is based on traditional and paternalistic modes (e.g. the Japanese use power not to dominate but to promote trust and reduce behavioural uncertainty) (Lin & Miller, 2003).

We must not neglect research on an aspect that relates to power in an international context and goes beyond the dyadic business relationship to significantly influence it, that is: power distance. Power distance, as a dimension of the national culture measurement instrument, was defined by Hofstede (2001, p. 98) as "the extent to which the less powerful members of institutions and organisations within a country expect and accept that power is distributed unequally", meaning that some people in a society or organisation have more power privileges than others, which is also accepted by the society or organisation (Drogendijk & Holm, 2012). This dimension has a great impact on hierarchy and dependency, and therefore affects the organisational structure within companies in certain societies (Soares et al., 2007). In societies with high power distance, power and wealth are concentrated in a few people at the top of the hierarchy who also make all the decisions, while people at other levels merely execute these decisions and accept the differences in power and wealth. The lower the power distance, the more people expect to participate in organisational decision-making. In other words, headquarters in cultures with high power distance are expected to control the actions of their subsidiaries because of their hierarchical position and the formal authority and centralised control derived from it. In this case, subsidiaries are expected to exercise authority. In contrast, subsidiaries from cultures with low power distance are more likely to disagree with power differentials based on formal hierarchical position, and to question the authority of the headquarters. Therefore, in such cultures, the headquarters is expected to consult with its subsidiaries or even award them autonomy to make their own decisions (Hofstede, 2001; Drogendijk & Holm, 2012).

Power distance is also related to conflict (discussed in the next subsection):

Lower power distances are associated with a degree of popular consensus that reduces the likelihood of disruptive conflict. In countries where power distance is higher, old power holders are less willing to relinquish their power, which may subsequently lead to a higher likelihood of conflict. On the high-power distance side, there is a latent conflict between the powerful and the powerless, a fundamental distrust that may never explode but is always present. On the low power distance side, the ideal model is harmony between the powerful and the powerless, which in practice may also be "latent", i.e. not excluding actual conflict, but pragmatic rather than fundamental.

(Hofstede, 2001)

Finally, conflict in business relationships in cultures with high power distance is said to be managed through the use of an avoidant or dominant conflict resolution style, while the use of a dominant style would be perceived negatively in collectivist cultures. There is also a high preference for a compromising and accommodating conflict resolution style in cultures with high uncertainty avoidance and long-term orientation (Gunkel et al., 2016).

Power distance has the most direct impact on organisational culture (Hewett et al., 2006). When Hofstede's culture dimensions are related to the organisational types of the cultures studied (the pyramid model for the French, who tend to resolve organisational conflicts by referring to hierarchy; the Village Market Model for Britons who tend to resolve them through horizontal negotiation; and the Well-Oiled Machine for Germans who resolve conflicts by establishing procedures), implicitly structured organisation is present in societies with low power distance and weak uncertainty avoidance; work-flow bureaucracy in countries with low power distance and strong uncertainty avoidance; and complete bureaucracy in societies with high power distance and strong uncertainty avoidance (Hofstede, 2001).

We can also draw a parallel between power and one of the latest conceptualisations of culture, the Yin Yang theory (Fang, 2012). Yin Yang, the Taoist philosophical principle of dualism, is represented by a circle evenly divided by a curved line into a black (yin) and a white (yang) part. Yin symbolises "female" energy, such as the moon, night, water, weakness, softness, passivity, darkness and femininity. Yang symbolises "male" energy, such as the sun, fire, day, strength, hardness, clarity, brightness, activity and masculinity. Together they symbolise the integration of two opposing cosmic energies, as do all universal phenomena according to this philosophy. More importantly, the white dot in the black part and the black dot in the white part show the coexistence and dynamic unity of opposites. Yin Yang is a Chinese philosophy and lifestyle that embraces paradoxes, dynamism and change (Fang, 2006, 2012). Similarly, in international business relationships, coercive and non-coercive, or mediated and non-mediated power coexist as two opposing sources of power that, according to Yin Yang theory, would be used differently depending on the situation, context and time.

3.2.3 Conflict and power in international business relationships

The word conflict is derived from the Latin word *configere*, meaning here a clash between a distribution channel member's behaviour and its international channel partner (Coughlan et al., 2006). We understand conflict in international business relations as "a condition or situation in which one channel member perceives another as an adversary who engages in behavior designed to destroy or thwart him or to gain resources at his expense" (Robicheaux & El-Ansary, 1975, p. 18). Conflict is synonymous with an overall level of disagreement in relationships, which is determined by the frequency, intensity and duration of the disagreement (Anderson & Narus, 1990). A positive relationship has been confirmed between channel member influence and conflict level, and conversely, a negative relationship has been confirmed between conflict and influence on other channel members (Gaski, 1984; Gaski & Ray, 2003). In summary, the greater a firm's influence on other channel members, the less conflict will occur because it is best for the other channel members to conform to the dominant firm (Anderson & Narus, 1990).

In essence, conflict behaviour is inherent and inevitable in distribution channels, as it results from functional (task) dependence in channel relationships, as well as a lack of consensus among channel members regarding their specific roles in the channel. The majority of traditional research views conflict as two-dimensional: task vs emotional, cognitive vs relational, or substantive vs affective. Content conflicts, also referred to as task conflicts (e.g. Jehn, 1997; Shoham, 1998), cognitive conflicts (e.g. Amason, 1996; Ohbuchi & Suzuki, 2003), and issue conflicts (e.g. Rahim, 2011), originate from disagreements about tasks, procedures, strategies, business ideas and other business-related issues. The resolution of such conflicts involves the evaluation of opinions and ideas based on logic, evidence and critical and innovative thinking. Therefore, this conflict has a positive functional and constructive connotation. Affective conflict, also referred to as emotional conflict (e.g. Shoham & Rose, 2007), relational conflict (e.g. Jehn, 1997), psychological conflict (e.g. Rahim, 2011) and interpersonal conflict (e.g. Ohbuchi & Suzuki, 2003), is caused by incompatible emotions and feelings about some or all issues between two social entities. The actions of one or both parties usually include personal attacks, personality conflicts, sarcasm, criticism and ridicule of the other's ideas, leading to distrust, anger, frustration and hostility in the relationship. The consequences of such conflicts are negative, so they have a dysfunctional or destructive connotation.

Similarly, power has a positive and a negative connotation. The negative connotations that describe power include exploitation, abuse, injustice, oppression, mistreatment and even brutality. From the perspective of international marketing channels, the negative use of power is manifested in actions that force a particular channel member to create value without receiving compensation for doing so. In contrast, the positive side of power is the potential to drive the channel toward a common goal, to achieve coordination of the channel and thereby lead to greater benefits for all channel members. Either way, the international marketing channel needs power to maximise the profits of the channel, which is not the same as maximising the profits of each individual member. In essence, channel members need to use power to defend themselves and promote better ways to achieve channel value (Coughlan et al., 2006).

The generally accepted understanding of the relationship between power and conflict in the existing literature (e.g. Pfajfar et al., 2019) postulates a positive relationship between coercive power and dysfunctional conflict, and non-coercive power and functional conflict, and vice versa (see Figure 3.7). Indeed, an international firm can reduce conflict by controlling and organising information sources (Lucas & Gresham, 1986), thereby creating information power. Furthermore, "mutual feelings of identification can prevent disagreement and conflict" (Raven & Kruglanski, 1970), while the use of referent power can be a basis for managing disagreement (Rawwas et al., 1997). When organisations face a changing heterogeneous environment, expert power has a greater effect on persuading channel members to follow them than threat or punishment (Lucas & Gresham, 1986). Moreover, expert power is a more important factor in resolving disputes than other sources of power without coercion (e.g. legitimate and referential sources of power) (Rawwas et al., 1997). Expert power can be an effective means of reducing

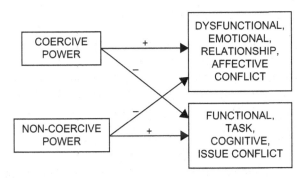

Figure 3.7 The relationship between power and conflict

conflict, but only if there is a high level of trust between the parties. The assumption is that the party who perceives another party as an expert is less likely to be involved in conflict because the expert's actions must be good for the entire channel (Lusch, 1976; Raven & Kruglanski, 1970). Empirical research suggests that the source of expert power has a significant and positive impact on constructive conflict (Rawwas et al., 1997). Previous research suggests that legitimate power could be used to manage conflict (Raven & Kruglanski, 1970), while it has also been found to increase conflict (Brown et al., 1983); if one party has the legitimate right to dictate behaviour to the other party, that party will engage in less and less intense conflict, supporting the suggestion that legitimate power can be used as an effective tool to reduce conflict (Lusch, 1976; Rawwas et al., 1997). Interestingly, reward power has not been found to directly lead to channel conflict, reducing dissatisfaction or an increase in channel performance (e.g. Gaski & Nevin, 1985; Lusch, 1976; Rawwas et al., 1997; Yavas, 1997), as conflict in this situation is less intense or even avoided because the other party feels that it cannot disagree with the influencing party due to the rewards it can offer (Lusch, 1976). The use of coercive power increases conflict in international distribution channels (e.g. Lusch, 1976; Brown et al., 1983; Gaski & Nevin, 1985; Yavas, 1997; Moore et al., 2004). A target may perceive the conflict resulting from the exercise of coercive power as more intense. By obeying the influencer, the target is faced with limited choices, which also increases the possibility of conflict (Zhuang et al., 2010), while the target may desire to retaliate and avoid the influencer as often as possible (Lusch, 1976). Moreover, there is empirical evidence for a positive and significant relationship between the source of coercive power and destructive conflict in distribution channels (Rawwas et al., 1997). In fact, some studies (e.g. Webb & Hogan, 2002) suggest that the use of coercive power significantly increases the likelihood of channel relationship failure because it induces negative attitudes toward the actors who use it (Korpi, 1985). Therefore, the use of coercive power is often seen as risky and counterproductive (Rawwas et al., 1997).

Information transfer between markets as a precursor to international conflict can be explained by transaction cost theory, one of the four basic components (along with agency theory, property rights and information economics) of the new theory of institutional economics. According to transaction cost theory, any exchange relationship involves imperfect (asymmetric) information, opportunistic behaviour by both partners and bounded rationality (Williamson, 1985). These factors create uncertainty, which in turn creates the potential for conflict. It has therefore been suggested that firms need to balance transaction costs against capabilities when making cross-border decisions (Madhok, 1998). Coughlan et al. (2006) use an interesting analogy to describe conflict. They compare assessing the level of conflict in channel relationships to taking a photograph. Similarly, conflict is compared to the process of shooting a film, as it consists of episodes or incidents. The authors explain that when the episodes or incidents are frequent, each new conflict is seen in a worse light. Conversely, conflict is interpreted positively when friction does not occur often.

Different marketing objectives guide channel members to perform planned and unplanned actions, as a result of which, in the absence of a high degree of cooperation or agreement among channel members, tension may occur. External factors that exacerbate these tensions include declining sales, intense competition, government regulation, technological change and consumer activism. At some point, an incident occurs (e.g. a confrontation between two parties) or the tension reaches a threshold where it cannot be contained. Rahim (2011) asserts that conflict can only occur when it exceeds a threshold level of intensity and is recognised as conflict by the parties involved. In his opinion, the threshold of intensity is the point at which the conflict can no longer be ignored. Since there are differences in the threshold of conflict awareness or conflict tolerance between individuals, some will experience the conflict earlier than others. Since the intensity of the flare-up cannot be sustained for long, conflict resolution strategies should be used (e.g. negotiation, mediation, etc.) or the level of conflict will slowly decrease but will remain unresolved. The final stage of the conflict may have behavioural or financial implications that affect the achievement of organisational goals, further affect their implementation, or even contribute to an increase/decrease in tension in the channel (Rosenberg, 1974).

Conflicts in international distribution channels have positive and negative effects. On the negative side, conflict leads to a decrease in sales efficiency and consequently higher costs. Resistance to resolving future conflicts and emotional disruption, as well as the damage caused by subjectivity and biased judgments, can also be considered as negative consequences. On the positive side, conflict can motivate managers to actively review activities, and it can serve as an indication of the need for change and the evaluation of management performance (Rosenberg, 1974). Consequently, conflict has led to approaches to conflict resolution. If we draw a parallel with game theory, we are dealing with three possible outcomes. Purely cooperative conflicts are called "coordination conflicts" or "positive-sum games" because they have positive outcomes for both parties, which is also known as the "win-win" approach in negotiation literature. In contrast, purely competitive conflicts are called "zero-sum games" or "negative-sum games" because positive outcomes for one party are offset by negative outcomes for the other party, which is also known in negotiation literature as the "win-lose" approach. However, most real-life conflicts are mixed and characterised by cooperative and competing interests, which are also known as coalition games or non-zero-sum games in the literature (Rahim, 2011). Win-lose and lose-lose conflict management methods have several distinct characteristics, such as orientation toward us-versus-them rather than us-versus-problem solving, with each side looking at problems from its own point of view rather than defining a problem in terms of common needs (Darling & Heller, 2011). In most cases, the parties define a conflict as a zero-sum game in which they seek to leverage different sources of power, when in fact it is a conflict of mixed motives (Deutsch, 1990).

International buyers and sellers are not at the same level of power and do not perceive distribution (tasks) in the same way. It has been found that buyers are more prevention oriented and focus on loss-related issues, while sellers are considered more promotion oriented and focus on profit-related issues. Therefore, in terms of positive outcomes, buyers feel better about not suffering losses and sellers feel better about making profits. From the perspective of negative outcomes, buyers will feel worse about losses and sellers will feel worse about lack of profits (Monga & Zhu, 2005). Not only are perceptual differences found between members of dyads, but contrary to general expectations, the relationship between an exporter from a developing country and an importer from a developed country is characterised by relatively low levels of conflict (Katsikeas & Piercy, 1991). When looking specifically at the emotional conflict that can arise from the buyer-seller relationship, it is important to determine which emotions are essential to the relationship. The extant research found that four positive emotions (pride, connectedness, empathy and emotional wisdom) and six negative emotions (guilt, shame, embarrassment, envy, jealousy and social anxiety) are critical to a successful buyer-seller relationship (Bagozzi, 2006). Price issues have been found to be the main cause of conflict between importers and exporters, suggesting that economic outcomes remain a fundamental principle for the establishment and development of trade relationships between parties (Katsikeas & Piercy, 1991). Since buyers and sellers react differently to price outcomes, they are like the two sides of a transaction coin that are together in a monetary exchange but do not have the same view (Monga & Zhu, 2005).

Power is a source of conflict, but at what level, when and in what context? Contextual factors of all kinds have been found to be more important sources of conflict than individual predispositions, suggesting that we need to go beyond individuals and individual departments to identify the sources of conflict (Barclay, 1991). Sources of conflict can be found at four different levels (Laine, 2002): the organisational level (power/dependence, organisational culture, role confusion), the individual level (incompatible perceptions, attitudes, values, preferences), the operational level (actors' perception of incompatibility of goals, degree of interdependence in activities, extent of sharing of necessary resources), and the external level (change in another relationship within the network). There have been several research attempts to postulate power as a source of conflict. Differences in members' perceptions of realities (e.g. dependence, power) in international channel dyads have been identified as a source of channel conflict (e.g. Etgar, 1978; Coughlan et al., 2001; Zhou et al., 2007). A study of US and Japanese business relationships found that the use of subtle power tends to minimise conflict, while aggressive power creates resistance and conflict (Johnson et al., 1990). "Conflict creates more conflict" (Coughlan et al., 2006). When the level of frustration and tension is high, it is difficult for channel members to move on without questioning their counterpart's commitment to the relationship. We should not neglect the intermediary's dependence on the manufacturer, especially for product and pricing decisions, as generating a high potential for conflict (Kotler et al., 2009).

The power of a channel member has often been empirically studied in relation to channel conflict. The first attempt was made by El-Ansary and Stern (1972), who failed to prove the relationship between a channel member's power and previous sources of power. In a study by Yavas (1997), no significant relationship between power bases and conflict was demonstrated as neither coercive nor non-coercive sources of power were significantly associated with conflict. However, coercive power was found to have a positive impact on conflict, while the relationship between non-coercive power and conflict was not significant (Zhuang et al., 2010). While the perceived use of power decreases constructive conflict, the suggestion that power increases destructive conflict is not empirically supported (Rawwas et al., 1997). The relationship between power and conflict has been empirically tested in relation to the environment (Lucas & Gresham, 1986). The authors found that channels operating in a homogeneous and stable task environment experience productive conflict only when there is a very low level of disagreement, while coercive power is the most appropriate and effective means of managing such conflict. However, when dealing with organisations operating in a changing heterogeneous environment, higher levels of conflict are recognised as productive and the use of non-coercive sources of power is most effective in dealing with conflict. In addition, levels of conflict are highest when reward and coercive power are used (Stern et al., 1973). In this context, a distinction must be made between aggressive forms of power (referred to by other lines of research as coercive, economic and mediating power) and non-aggressive forms of power, with the former tending to increase conflict and the latter tending to decrease it (Lee, 2001). Indeed, power is most evident in conflicts that arise over issues related to important decisions rather than routine operations (Korpi, 1985).

Nevertheless, we can conclude that the impact of power on conflict depends primarily on the source of power, as "the use of coercive power promotes conflict at a significantly higher rate than the use of non-coercive power" (Tikoo, 2005, p. 332). SMEs have limited power and a small resource base in their relationships with larger firms, so sources of conflict may be firm-size specific. Therefore, the main sources of conflict for SMEs include cultural differences, product or service quality, and financial aspects of collaboration, with the application of positive conflict resolution styles being particularly difficult (Ratajczak-Mrozek et al., 2019). Finally, the majority of the existing literature focuses on dyadic relationships, while the study of conflict and power in network relationships is rare. Looking at conflict in the context of networks gives the researcher or firm the opportunity to trace the roots of a dyadic relationship conflict in other relationships, and to see how they are interconnected. Thus, the causes of conflict may depend on the connections in the network, while addressing conflict may require changes in other relationships in the network (in other words, dyads other than the dyadic relationship in which the conflict originally occurred) (Welch & Wilkinson, 2005).

Power has important consequences for international relations because of conflict. On the one hand, power can be used in a coercive way, meaning that both parties can easily switch to another partner when conflicts arise and escalate. On the other hand, power can also be used in a cooperative way, which leads to the establishment of shared norms and expectations as well as prosperous relations in the future (Gadde et al., 2010). Furthermore, the use of sanctions as a method of conflict resolution is considered an extreme, often ineffective means of conflict resolution (Moore et al., 2004). However, it represents the first step in moving towards more collaborative methods of decision-making. A positive outcome of functional conflict is seen as a more balanced distribution of power in channel relationships (Rosenberg, 1974; Dwyer et al., 1987; Coughlan et al., 2006; Rahim, 2011). Functional conflict is much more likely when a downstream channel member has more power and influence over its supplier, as the influential party is usually the contending party and drives the channel to outperform its competitors. Channel conflict can affect the overall performance of the channel, as it usually occurs when the actions of a channel member prevent the channel from achieving its goals. This happens (usually) due to the interdependence existing between all channel members (Coughlan et al., 2006). However, poor channel performance does not necessarily have to be due to channel conflicts, but can also be to the result of poor channel design. The task of a channel manager is to recognise and distinguish between these two possibilities.

International channel conflicts can be resolved by applying one or more sources of channel performance. In general, conflict resolution strategies are closely related to reward power in international channels, which encourages the reseller not to abandon sales efforts when another reseller is competing, as the first reseller could be compensated for its efforts if it wins a sale (Coughlan et al., 2006). In considering conflict resolution styles, we can draw a parallel with negotiation styles, where each party chooses between different levels of assertiveness (i.e. how concerned they are with achieving their own goals) and cooperativeness (i.e. how concerned they are with the other party's goals). Based on these two dimensions, we arrive at several conflict resolution styles and different sources of power that can be used in the process (see Figure 3.8). Avoidance is a strategy used by a channel member who is relatively passive or has no power (Coughlan et al., 2006).

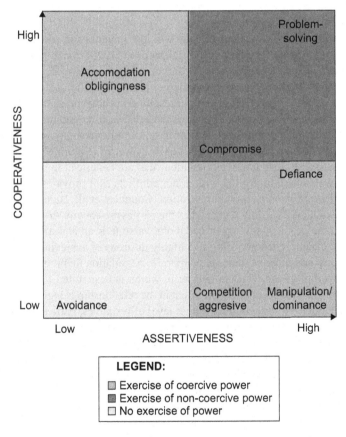

Figure 3.8 Connection between power and conflict resolution styles

Source: Adapted from Thomas, 1992; Oliver, 1991; Rahim et al., 2001; Coughlan et al., 2006; Gadde et al., 2010.

The avoidance strategy can take two forms, either suppressing the conflict or withdrawing from the issues causing the conflict by letting fate solve the problems rather than making things happen (Richardson, 1995). Adaptation is another way of keeping the peace. However, unlike avoidance, it is an active strategy that focuses on the other party's goals rather than your own. It is a way of strengthening a relationship as it promotes reciprocity, thus building trust and commitment in the long run. However, if the relationship lacks commitment, reciprocity will most likely fail, and this strategy of conflict resolution will lead to the party being exploited (Coughlan et al., 2006). In this case, the use of coercive force can align the goals of international business partners and lead them out of conflict. Competition or aggression is the exact opposite of accommodation as one party focuses on their own goals and neglects the goals of the other party. Therefore, this strategy is also referred to as a zero-sum game.

Conflict can be associated with the win-lose mentality, in which one side seeks to dominate the relationship (Richardson, 1995). Since this strategy promotes distrust and exacerbates conflict, it is not appropriate when seeking long-term relationships (Coughlan et al., 2006). The use of power is usually evident in this type of conflict resolution behaviour, as the dominant party uses coercive power to control the relationship, leading to compliance rather than commitment. However, this conflict resolution style is not appropriate when both parties are equally powerful (Rahim, 2011). Compromise is a strategy that seeks solutions that are beneficial to both parties, and is well suited to dealing with minor conflicts as it provides the easiest and quickest route to a mutual resolution (Coughlan et al., 2006). This conflict resolution style only works when the parties are equally strong (Rahim, 2011). The problem-solving or collaborative style is an ambitious style in that the channel member using it is highly desirous of achieving both their own goals and those of their counterpart. In negotiation literature, this style is referred to as the win-win approach, which is best suited for resolving conflict when the level of commitment in the relationship is high. However, the collaborative style requires a high level of resources, particularly information, time and energy. In addition, problem-solving usually requires the disclosure of sensitive information that could be used against you later in the negotiation or channel relationship (Coughlan et al., 2006). Therefore, this style is often used when the dependency in the distribution channel is low (Dant & Schul, 1992). In this case, the members of the international distribution channel do not exercise coercive power to achieve positive outcomes for both parties involved in the relationship. Since conflicts differ from country to country, regional offices should be able to resolve conflicts at the local level (Rosenberg, 1974). It has been shown that more powerful parties prefer low-risk strategies as these are aimed at immediate maximum self-gain and provide them with scope for tactical manoeuvring and greater influence over the weaker party. However, in the case of high dependence in the channel and in disputes where the stakes are high, have political connotations and are complex, third party intervention is preferred (Dant & Schul, 1992). In summary, managing power and conflict in the manner described above has a positive impact on export performance, which we discuss in more detail in the next subsection.

3.2.4 Handling power for managing export performance in international business relationships

Export performance is one of the most widely studied constructs in international marketing literature. Its sources include conflict (e.g. Cadogan et al., 2003), resources and capabilities (e.g. Morgan et al., 2004), the degree of internationalisation (e.g. Papadopoulos & Martin, 2010) and international marketing strategy (e.g. Katsikeas et al., 2000). We consider export performance as "the composite result of a firm's international sales" (Shoham, 1998, p. 61) which serves as a guide for firms to evaluate their success on the domestic and international arena (Lages, 2000). In the history of export development, many other facets of export performance have been studied. For example, the export marketing strategy of American manufacturers is determined by both internal forces (e.g. product and firm characteristics) and external forces (e.g. export market and industry characteristics), with export marketing strategy (e.g. price competitiveness and marketing mix adjustment) playing an important role (Cavusgil & Zou, 1994). However, the history of thinking about export performance faced a division of theories into two rival theoretical streams (La et al., 2005). The first theoretical stream is known as the behavioural perspective (Leonidou et al., 2002), while the second is recognised as the relational approach (Styles & Ambler, 2000). The latter explores the nature and effects of exporter-overseas distributor relationships, and power in particular.

Export performance has been conceptualised and operationalised in a variety of ways (Das, 1994; Lages, 2000). The existing literature distinguishes between financial (e.g. profit, sales revenues, market share) and non-financial measurements of success (e.g. satisfaction with export venture, goal achievement) (Zou & Stan, 1998). In most studies, financial assessment is associated with objective terms (e.g. absolute numbers or percentages), while non-financial assessment is associated with subjective terms (e.g. export (marketing) managers' perceptions) (Lages, 2000). Only the use of non-financial evaluation at the international level has seen an increase (Das, 1994; Lages, 2000; Shoham, 1996). In particular, export firm satisfaction as a non-financial measurement of export performance has taken a special place in the literature, overcoming some of the limitations associated with the exclusive use of financial measurements (Lages, 2000). In order to capture the full complexity of export performance, taking into account numerous environmental and organisational factors, it is advisable to use assessment based on a combination of financial and non-financial measurements (Bijmolt & Zwart, 1994; Zou & Stan, 1998; Shoham, 1998; Lages, 2000; Lages et al., 2005).

The effect of the components of relationships on export performance has been studied by scholars, who have made theoretical and empirical contributions to the literature on international business relationships (e.g. Leonidou & Kaleka, 1998; Mainela, 2001; Styles & Ambler, 2004; Leonidou, 2004). The effect of power on export performance has been studied either directly or through a mediator, with the latter predominating in existing research. For example, international marketing channel performance is an outcome of the "effectiveness of channel control and channel members' satisfaction or dissatisfaction with the channel relationship" (Robicheaux & El-Ansary, 1975), where channel control is understood as the result of channel members' exercised power. Since the relationship determined by the use of power is considered to consist of low cooperation, high levels of conflict and distorted communication (Lusch & Brown, 1996), these conditions hinder export market orientation. Consequently, the empirical findings confirm that power is negatively related to export market orientation behaviour, which in turn is positively related to export performance (Chang & Fang, 2015). In other words, the more market-oriented the exporting firm is, the more power it has over its main foreign distributor, which in turn has an impact on export performance and exporter satisfaction (Racela et al., 2007). The use of independent incentives (attributable to channel members' power) as the main mediator of channel relationship commitment has been found to determine international channel performance. Such relationship-enhancing incentives, as opposed to contractual incentives, promote channel commitment more effectively, leading to better channel performance (Sheu & Hu, 2009). Finally, coercive power (on the exporter and importer side) and non-coercive power (only on the exporter side) are indirectly related to performance through dysfunctional and functional conflicts in international relationships (Pfajfar et al., 2019).

Direct links between power and export performance have also been tested. A study examining how Chinese distributors perceive the use of power sources by international joint venture suppliers found a direct positive relationship between non-coercive power and relationship satisfaction, and a direct negative relationship between coercive power and relationship satisfaction. Moreover, indirect relationships are mediated by conflict (coercive power is positively related to conflict, while non-coercive power is negatively related), which has a negative effect on the relationship satisfaction of the Chinese distributor in the international joint venture (Lee, 2001). In terms of the franchisor-franchisee relationship, franchisors who rely more on non-coercive sources of power and less on coercive sources of power have franchisees who are more satisfied with the franchise relationship (Hunt & Nevin, 1974). Coercive and reward power exercised directly and indirectly influence relationship performance through procedural and distributive justice (Hoppner et al., 2014). Finally, an inverted U-shaped relationship exists between the concentration of power and MNC performance (Lee, 2021).

The impact of power on export performance has also been tested in the context of international negotiations. If power plays an important role in international negotiations between suppliers and buyers where product attributes, logistics or merchandising are being negotiated, it is also crucial in price setting. An exporting manufacturer that has strong power can obtain better (higher) prices for its products, resulting in increasing export revenues and improved export profitability (Pham & Petersen, 2021). Suppliers with strong power have been found to use "non-mediated" approaches (information exchange and recommendations) and rely less on "mediated" tactics like threats and "legalistic appeals" in their business relationships, with the latter tactics having a negative impact on performance and the former having a positive impact (Boyle & Dwyer, 1995). The power of the exporting manufacturer (as a member of a global supply chain) depends on functional upgrade initiatives (i.e. product development, distribution, sales promotion) and initiatives in the negotiation process (i.e. improving negotiation skills and market knowledge), which enhance its export performance (Pham & Petersen, 2021). Interestingly, experience with one type of channel and channel power were not required to succeed in international digital channels (Wolk & Skiera, 2009).

3.2.5 Summary

This chapter focuses on culture and conflict as antecedents to power and export performance as a result of the use of power in international business relationships. Cultural and power distance have been identified as critical to international business relationships, particularly headquarters-subsidiary relationships and conflict resolution strategies. The types and sources of conflict were also analysed. Based on previous research, we propose that coercive power negatively affects functional conflict and positively affects dysfunctional conflict, while non-coercive power positively affects functional conflict and negatively affects dysfunctional conflict. Conflict resolution strategies are ranked according to the assertiveness and cooperativeness of international business partners, and the link to the types of power exercised has been established. Finally, we have reviewed studies that examined the relationship between power and export performance in the context of international marketing channels and international business negotiations.

Note

1 This chapter builds on the discussion in Pfajfar, G. (2012). *The gap between buyers and sellers and its influence on conflict within international distribution channels: Doctoral dissertation*, available at www.cek.ef.uni-lj.si/doktor/pfajfar.pdf.

3.3 References

Amason, A. C. (1996). Distinguishing the effects of functional and dysfunctional conflict on strategic decision making: Resolving a paradox for top management teams. *Academy of Management Journal*, 39(1), 123–148.

Ambos, B., Asakawa, K., & Ambos, T. C. (2011). A dynamic perspective on subsidiary autonomy. *Global Strategy Journal*, 1(3–4), 301–316.

Anderson, J. C., & Narus, J. A. (1990). A model of distributor firm and manufacturer firm working partnerships. *Journal of Marketing*, 54(1), 42–58.

Axelsson, B., & Agndal, H. (2000). *Internationalization of the firm. A note on the crucial role of the individual's contact network. Or fragments to a theory of individual's relationship sediments and opportunity networks as driving forces and enablers of internationalization*. In 16th IMP conference, Bath, UK, pp. 7–9.

Bagozzi, R. (2006). The role of social and self-conscious emotions in the regulation of B2B relationships in salesperson-customer interactions. *Journal of Business & Industrial Marketing*, 21(7), 453–457.

Barclay, D. W. (1991). Interdepartmental conflict in organizational buying-the impact of the organizational context. *Journal of Marketing Research*, 28(2), 145–159.

Bartlett, C. A., & Ghoshal, S. (1986). Tap your subsidiaries for global reach. *Harvard Business Review*, 64(6), 87–94.

Bijmolt, T. H., & Zwart, P. S. (1994). The impact of internal factors on the export success of Dutch small and medium-sized firms. *Journal of Small Business Management*, 32(2), 69–83.

Birkinshaw, J., Holm, U., Thilenius, P., & Arvidsson, N. (2000). Consequences of perception gaps in the headquarters–subsidiary relationship. *International Business Review*, 9(3), 321–344.

Black, P. W., & Avruch, K. (1993). Culture, power and international negotiations: Understanding Palau-US status negotiations. *Millennium*, 22(3), 379–400.

Bouquet, C., & Birkinshaw, J. (2008). Weight versus voice: How foreign subsidiaries gain attention from corporate headquarters. *Academy of Management Journal*, 51(3), 577–601.

Boyle, B. A., & Dwyer, F. R. (1995). Power, bureaucracy, influence, and performance: Their relationships in industrial distribution channels. *Journal of Business Research*, 32(3), 189–200.

Brown, J. R., Lusch, R. F., & Muehling, D. D. (1983). Conflict and power dependence relations in retailer supplier channels. *Journal of Retailing*, 59(4), 53–80.

Cadogan, J. W., Diamantopoulos, A., & Siguaw, J. A. (2003). Export market oriented activities: Their antecedents and performance consequences. *Journal of International Business Studies*, 33(3), 615–626.

Carr, M. (2002). *Cultural stereotyping in international business relationships.* 18th Annual Conference of the Industrial Marketing and Purchasing Group, Perth, 1–14.

Cavusgil, S. T., & Zou, S. (1994). Marketing strategy-performance relationship: An investigation of the empirical link in export market ventures. *Journal of Marketing*, 58(1), 1–21.

Chang, Y. S., & Fang, S. R. (2015). Enhancing export performance for business markets: Effects of interorganizational relationships on export market orientation (EMO). *Journal of Business-to-Business Marketing*, 22(3), 211–228.

Coughlan, A. T., Anderson, E., Stern, L. W., & El-Ansary, A. I. (2006). *Marketing Channels*. 7th ed. Upper Saddle River: Pearson.

Cuervo-Cazurra, A., Mudambi, R., & Pedersen, T. (2019). Subsidiary power: Loaned or owned? The lenses of agency theory and resource dependence theory. *Global Strategy Journal*, 9(4), 491–501.

Dant, R. P., & Schul, P. L. (1992). Conflict resolution processes in contractual channels of distribution. *Journal of Marketing*, 56(1), 38–54.

Darling, J. R., & Heller, V. L. (2011). Managing conflict with the Chinese: The Key from an in-depth single case study. *Chinese Management Studies*, 5(1), 35–54.

Das, M. (1994). Successful and unsuccessful exporters from developing countries: Some preliminary findings. *European Journal of Marketing*, 28(12), 19–33.

Datu, J. A. D., & Reyes, J. A. S. (2015). The dark side of possessing power: Power reduces happiness in a collectivist context. *Social Indicators Research*, 124(3), 981–991.

De Ruyter, K., Wetzels, M., & Lemmink, J. (1996). The power of perceived service quality in international marketing channels. *European Journal of Marketing*, 30(12), 22–38.

Deutsch, M. (1990). Sixty years of conflict. *The International Journal of Conflict Management*, 1(3), 237–263.

Dörrenbächer, C., & Gammelgaard, J. (2011). Subsidiary power in multinational corporations: The subtle role of micro-political bargaining power. *Critical Perspectives on International Business*, 7(1), 30–47.

Dörrenbächer, C., & Gammelgaard, J. (2016). Subsidiary initiative taking in multinational corporations: The relationship between power and issue selling. *Organization Studies*, 37(9), 1249–1270.

Drogendijk, R., & Holm, U. (2015). Cultural distance or cultural positions? Analysing the effect of culture on the HQ–subsidiary relationship. In *Knowledge, networks and power* (pp. 366–392). London: Palgrave Macmillan.

Dwyer, F. R., Schurr, P. H., & Oh, S. (1987). Developing buyer-seller relationships. *Journal of Marketing*, 51(2), 11–27.

El-Ansary, A. I., & Stern, L. W. (1972). Power measurement in the distribution channel. *Journal of Marketing Research*, 9(1), 47–52.

Etgar, M. (1978). Intrachannel conflict and use of power. *Journal of Marketing Research*, 40, 273–274.

Fang, T. (2006). Negotiation: The Chinese style. *Journal of Business & Industrial Marketing*, 21(1), 50–60.

Fang, T. (2012). Yin Yang: A new perspective on culture. *Management and Organization Review*, 8(1), 25–50.

Gadde, L.-E., Håkansson, H., & Persson, G. (2010). *Supply networks strategies*. 2nd ed. Chichester: Wiley.

Gaski, J. F. (1984). The theory of power and conflict in channels of distribution. *Journal of Marketing*, 48(3), 9–29.

Gaski, J. F., & Nevin, J. R. (1985). The differential effects of exercised and unexercised power sources in a marketing channel. *Journal of Marketing Research*, 22(2), 130–142.

Gaski, J. F., & Ray, N. M. (2004). Alienation in the distribution channel-conceptualization, measurement, theory testing. *International Journal of Physical Distribution & Logistics Management*, 34(2), 158–200.

Ghoshal, S., & Nohria, N. (1989). Internal differentiation within multinational corporations. *Strategic Management Journal*, 10(4), 323–337.

Gunkel, M., Schlaegel, C., & Taras, V. (2016). Cultural values, emotional intelligence, and conflict handling styles: A global study. *Journal of World Business*, 51(4), 568–585.

Gupta, A. K., & Govindarajan, V. (1991). Knowledge flows and the structure of control within multinational corporations. *Academy of Management Review*, 16(4), 768–792.

Hewett, K., Money, R. B., & Sharma, S. (2006). National culture and industrial buyer-seller relationships in the United States and Latin America. *Journal of the Academy of Marketing Science*, 34(3), 386–402.

Hingley, M., Angell, R., & Lindgreen, A. (2015). The current situation and future conceptualization of power in industrial markets. *Industrial Marketing Management*, 48, 226–230.

Hofstede, G. (2001). *Culture's consequences: Comparing values, behaviors, institutions and organizations across nations*. Thousand Oaks, CA: Sage Publications.

Hoppner, J. J., Griffith, D. A., & Yeo, C. (2014). The intertwined relationships of power, justice and dependence. *European Journal of Marketing*, 48(9/10), 1690–1708.

Hunt, S. D., & Nevin, J. R. (1974). Power in a channel of distribution: Sources and consequences. *Journal of Marketing Research*, 11(2), 186–193.

Jap, S. D., & Ganesan, S. (2000). Control mechanisms and the relationship life cycle: Implications for safeguarding specific investments and developing commitment. *Journal of Marketing Research*, 37(2), 227–245.

Jehn, K. A. (1997). A qualitative analysis of conflict types and dimensions in organizational groups. *Administrative Science Quarterly*, 530–557.

Johnson, J. L., Sakano, T., Cote, J. A., & Onzo, N. (1993). The exercise of interfirm power and its repercussions in US-Japanese channel relationships. *Journal of Marketing*, 57(2), 1–10.

Johnson, J. L., Sakano, T., & Onzo, N. (1990). Behavioral relations in across-culture distribution systems: Influence, control and conflict in US Japanese marketing channels. *Journal of International Business Studies*, 21(4), 639–655.

Kaleka, A., Piercy, N. F., & Katsikeas, C. S. (1997). The impact of level of company export development on exercised power in relationships between manufacturers and overseas distributors. *Journal of Marketing Management*, 13(1–3), 119–134.

Katsikeas, C. S., Goode, M. M., & Katsikea, E. (2000). Sources of power in international marketing channels. *Journal of Marketing Management*, 16(1–3), 185–202.

Katsikeas, C. S., Leonidou, L. C., & Morgan, N. A. (2000). Firm-level export performance assessment–review, evaluation and development. *Academy of Marketing Science Journal*, 28(4), 493–511.

Katsikeas, C. S., & Piercy, N. F. (1991). The relationship between exporters from a developing country and importers based in a developed country: Conflict considerations. *European Journal of Marketing*, 25(1), 6–25.

Katsikeas, C. S., & Piercy, N. F. (1992). Exporter-importer and exporter-domestic customer relationships: Power considerations. *Management Decision*, 30(4), 12–19.

Kopelman, S., Hardin, A. E., Myers, C. G., & Tost, L. P. (2016). Cooperation in multicultural negotiations: How the cultures of people with low and high power interact. *Journal of Applied Psychology*, 101(5), 721–730.

Korpi, W. (1985). Power resources approach vs. action and conflict: On causal and intentional explanations in the study of power. *Sociological Theory*, 3(2), 31–45.

Kostova, T., Marano, V., & Tallman, S. (2016). Headquarters–subsidiary relationships in MNCs: Fifty years of evolving research. *Journal of World Business*, 51(1), 176–184.

Kotler, P., Keller, K. L., Brady, M., Goodman, M., & Hansen, T. (2009a). *Marketing management*. Upper Saddle River, NJ: Pearson/Prentice Hall.

La, V. Q., Patterson, P. G., & Styles, C. W. (2005). Determinants of export performance across service types: A conceptual model. *Journal of Services Marketing*, 19(6), 379–391.

LaBahn, D. W., & Harich, K. R. (1997). Sensitivity to national business culture: Effects on US-Mexican channel relationship performance. *Journal of International Marketing*, 5(4), 29–51.

Lages, L. F. (2000). A conceptual framework of the determinants of export performance: Reorganizing key variables and shifting contingencies in export marketing. *Journal of Global Marketing*, 13(3), 29–51.

Lages, L. F., Lages, C., & Lages, C. R. (2005). Bringing export performance metrics into annual reports: The APEV scale and the PERFEX scorecard. *Journal of International Marketing*, 13(3), 79–104.

Laine, A. (2002). *Sources of conflict in cooperation between competitors*. In Proceedings from the 18th IMP conference. Dijon, France, pp. 1–26.

Lee, D. Y. (2001). Power, conflict and satisfaction in IJV supplier–Chinese distributor channels. *Journal of Business Research*, 52(2), 149–160.

Lee, J. M. (2021). MNCs as dispersed structures of power: Performance and management implications of power distribution in the subsidiary portfolio. *Journal of International Business Studies*, 1–30.

Leonidou, C. L. (2004). Industrial manufacturer-customer relationships: The discriminating role of the buying situation. *Industrial Marketing Management*, 33, 731–742.

Leonidou, L. C., Aykol, B., Spyropoulou, S., & Christodoulides, P. (2019). The power roots and drivers of infidelity in international business relationships. *Industrial Marketing Management*, 78, 198–212.

Leonidou, L. C., & Kaleka, A. A. (1998). Behavioural aspects of international buyer-seller relationships: Their association with export involvement. *International Marketing Review*, 373–397.

Leonidou, L., & Katsikeas, C. (2003). The role of foreign customer influences in building relationships with US exporting SMEs. *Long Range Planning*, 36(3), 227–252.

Leonidou, L. C., Katsikeas, C. S., & Samiee, S. (2002). Marketing strategy determinants of export performance: A meta-analysis. *Journal of Business Research*, 55(1), 51–67.

Leonidou, L. C., Talias, M. A., & Leonidou, C. N. (2008). Exercised power as a driver of trust and commitment in cross-border industrial buyer–seller relationships. *Industrial Marketing Management*, 37(1), 92–103.

Lin, X., & Miller, S. J. (2003). Negotiation approaches: Direct and indirect effect of national culture. *International Marketing Review*, 20(3), 286–303.

Lucas, G. H., & Gresham, L. G. (1986). Power, conflict, control and the application of contingency theory. *Journal of Academy of Marketing Science*, 13(3), 25–39.

Lusch, R. F. (1976). Channel conflict–its impact on retailer operating performance. *Journal of Retailing*, 52(2), 3–12.

Lusch, R. F., & Brown, J. R. (1996). Interdependency, contracting, and relational behavior in marketing channels. *Journal of Marketing*, 60(4), 19–38.

Madhok, A. (1998). The nature of multinational firm boundaries: Transaction cost, firm capabilities and foreign market entry mode. *International Business Review*, 7, 259–290.

Magee, J. C., & Smith, P. K. (2013). The social distance theory of power. *Personality and Social Psychology Review*, 17(2), 158–186.

Mainela, T. (2001). *Networks and social relationships in management of international joint ventures*. 17th Annual Conference of the Industrial Marketing and Purchasing Group, Oslo, pp. 1–21.

Malik, T. H., & Yazar, O. H. (2016). The negotiator's power as enabler and cultural distance as inhibitor in the international alliance formation. *International Business Review*, 25(5), 1043–1052.

Matanda, M. J., & Freeman, S. (2009). Effect of perceived environmental uncertainty on exporter–importer inter-organisational relationships and export performance improvement. *International Business Review*, 18(1), 89–107.

Monga, A., & Zhu, R. J. (2005). Buyers versus sellers: How they differ in their responses to framed outcomes. *Journal of Consumer Psychology*, 15(4), 325–333.

Moore, C. M., Birtwistle, G., & Burt, S. (2004). Channel power, conflict and conflict resolution in international fashion retailing. *European Journal of Marketing*, 38(7), 749–769.

Morgan, N. A., Kaleka, A., & Katsikeas, C. S. (2004). Antecedents of export venture performance: A theoretical model and empirical assessment. *Journal of Marketing*, 68(1), 90–108.

Mudambi, R., & Navarra, P. (2015). Is knowledge power? Knowledge flows, subsidiary power and rent-seeking within MNCs. In *The eclectic paradigm* (pp. 157–191). London: Palgrave Macmillan.

Mudambi, R., Pedersen, T., & Andersson, U. (2014). How subsidiaries gain power in multinational corporations. *Journal of World Business*, 49(1), 101–113.

Najafi-Tavani, Z., Zaefarian, G., Naudé, P., & Giroud, A. (2015). Reverse knowledge transfer and subsidiary power. *Industrial Marketing Management*, 48, 103–110.

Nyaga, G. N., Lynch, D. F., Marshall, D., & Ambrose, E. (2013). Power asymmetry, adaptation and collaboration in dyadic relationships involving a powerful partner. *Journal of Supply Chain Management*, 49(3), 42–65.

Ohbuchi, K. I., & Suzuki, M. (2003). Three dimensions of conflict issues and their effects on resolution strategies in organizational settings. *International Journal of Conflict Management*, 14(1), 61–73.

Oliver, C. (1991). Strategic responses to institutional processes. *Academy of Management Review*, 16(1), 145–179.

Papadopoulos, N., & Martín, O. M. (2010). Toward a model of the relationship between internationalization and export performance. *International Business Review*, 19(4), 388–406.

Pfajfar, G., Shoham, A., Brenčič, M. M., Koufopoulos, D., Katsikeas, C. S., & Mitręga, M. (2019). Power source drivers and performance outcomes of functional and dysfunctional conflict in exporter–importer relationships. *Industrial Marketing Management*, 78, 213–226.

Pham, H. S. T., & Petersen, B. (2021). The bargaining power, value capture, and export performance of Vietnamese manufacturers in global value chains. *International Business Review*, 101829.

Phookan, H., & Sharma, R. R. (2021). Subsidiary power, cultural intelligence and interpersonal knowledge transfer between subsidiaries within the multinational enterprise. *Journal of International Management*, 27(4), 100859.

Racela, O. C., Chaikittisilpa, C., & Thoumrungroje, A. (2007). Market orientation, international business relationships and perceived export performance. *International Marketing Review*, 24(2), 144–163.

Rahim, M. A. (2011). *Managing conflict in organizations*. 4th ed. New Jersey: Transaction Publishers.

Rahim, M. A., Antonioni, D., & Psenicka, C. (2001). A structural equations model of leader power, subordinates' styles of handling conflict, and job performance. *International Journal of Conflict Management*, 12(3), 191–211.

Ratajczak-Mrozek, M., Fonfara, K., & Hauke-Lopes, A. (2019). Conflict handling in small firms' foreign business relationships. *Journal of Business & Industrial Marketing*, 6(2), 171–183.

Raven, B. H., & Kruglanski, A. W. (1970). Conflict and power. In *The Structure of Conflict* (pp. 69–109).

Raven, P., Tansuhaj, P., & McCullough, J. (1993). Effects of power in export channels. *Journal of Global Marketing*, 7(2), 97–116.

Rawwas, M. Y., Vitell, S. J., & Barnes, J. H. (1997). Management of conflict using individual power sources: A retailers' perspective. *Journal of Business Research*, 40(1), 49–64.

Richardson, J. (1995). Avoidance as an active mode of conflict resolution. *An International Journal of Team Performance Management*, 1(4), 19–25.

Robicheaux, R. A., & El-Ansary, A. I. (1975). A general model for understanding channel member behavior. *Journal of Retailing*, 42(4), 13–30.

Rose, G. M., Shoham, A., Neill, S., & Ruvio, A. (2007). Manufacturer perceptions of the consequences of task and emotional conflict within domestic channels of distribution. *Journal of Business Research*, 60(4), 296–304.

Rosenberg, L. J. (1974). A new approach to distribution conflict management. *Business Horizons*, 67–75.

Sheu, J. B., & Hu, T. L. (2009). Channel power, commitment and performance toward sustainable channel relationship. *Industrial Marketing Management*, 38(1), 17–31.

Shoham, A. (1998). Export performance: A conceptualization and empirical assessment. *Journal of International Marketing*, 6(3), 59–81.

Soares, A. M., Farhangmehr, M., & Shoham, A. (2007). Hofstede's dimensions of culture in international marketing studies. *Journal of Business Research*, 60, 277–284.

Stern, L. W., Schultz, R. A., & Graber, J. R. (1973). The power base-conflict relationship: Preliminary findings. *Social Science Quarterly*, 54, 412–419.

Styles, C., & Ambler, T. (2000). The impact of relational variables on export performance: An empirical investigation in Australia and the UK. *Australian Journal of Management*, 25(3), 261–281.

Thomas, K. W. (1992). Conflict and conflict management–reflections and update. *Journal of Organizational Behavior*, 13(3), 265–274.

Tikoo, S. (2005). Franchisor use of influence and conflict in a business format franchise system. *International Journal of Retail and Distribution Management*, 33(5), 329–342.

Trang, N. T., Barrett, N. J., & Tho, N. D. (2003). *Cultural sensitivity and its impact on business relationship quality*. In 19th Annual Industrial Marketing and Purchasing Group Conference, Lugano, pp. 4–6.

Wang, N., Hua, Y., Wu, G., Zhao, C., & Wang, Y. (2019). Reverse transfer of innovation and subsidiary power: A moderated mediation model. *Journal of Business Research*, 103, 328–337.

Webb, K. L., & Hogan, J. E. (2002). Hybrid channel conflict: Causes and effects on channel performance. *Journal of Business & Industrial Marketing*, 17(5), 338–356.

Welch, C., & Wilkinson, I. (2005). Network perspectives on interfirm conflict: Reassessing a critical case in international business. *Journal of Business Research*, 58(2), 205–213.

Williamson, O. E. (1985). *The economic institutions of capitalism*. New York: Free Press.

Wolk, A., & Skiera, B. (2009). Antecedents and consequences of Internet channel performance. *Journal of Retailing and Consumer Services*, 16, 163–173.

Yamin, M., & Forsgren, M. (2006). Hymer's analysis of the multinational organization: Power retention and the demise of the federative MNE. *International Business Review*, 15(2), 166–179.

Yavas, U. (1997). The bases of power in international channels. *International Marketing Review*, 15(2), 143–158.

Zeng, F., Ye, Q., Dong, M. C., Huang, Z., & Liu, Z. (2020). Legitimizing actions in dependence-asymmetry relationships: A comparison between Chinese and Western firms. *Industrial Marketing Management*, 88, 163–172.

Zhou, N., Zhuang, G., & Yip, L. S. C. (2007). Perceptual difference of dependence and its impact on conflict in marketing channels in China: An empirical study with two-sided data. *Industrial Marketing Management*, 36(3), 309–321.

Zhuang, G., Xi, Y., & Tsang, A. S. (2010). Power, conflict, and cooperation: The impact of guanxi in Chinese marketing channels. *Industrial Marketing Management*, 39(1), 137–149.

Zou, S., & Stan, S. (1998). The determinants of export performance: A review of the empirical literature between 1987 and 1997. *International Marketing Review*, 15(5), 333–356.

Conclusions and implications

Conclusions

In this book, we have explored and provided clearer insights into the complexity of the key concept of power in business relationships, with an emphasis on the buyer-supplier type of relationship. In understanding power notion in inter-organisational settings, we build on classic definitions (Emerson, 1962; Dahl, 1957) that focus on social exchange and inter-individual relationships within groups and organisations. In the context of business relationships, we understand power in a manner similar to Cowan et al. (2015) as the potential of one actor to influence the behaviour of another actor when the former's expectations are inconsistent with the desires of the latter and the latter actor shows resistance. We have shown that the power within the relationship networks between buyers and suppliers can be a positive (e.g. Hingley, 2005) or a negative (Wolfe & McGinn, 2005) factor in maximising the benefits of the relationship parties. Based on the literature, we examined the nature of power as a building block of business relationships and the power-related tactics, especially from the weaker side of an asymmetric relationship. An extended analysis of Siemieniako and Mitręga (2018a) findings, as well as the results of our primary research (subsection 2.2), allowed us to distinguish power related intentional (Oukes et al., 2019) tactics as focal events and contextual events regarding power dynamics (Makkonen et al., 2012, 2021). Contextual events represent different sets of non-intentional tactics and external factors regarding the focal relationship and their impact on the power dynamics in the buyer-supplier relationship. Because we view power asymmetry in business-to-business relationships as a complex and multifaceted concept, we placed particular emphasis on a perceptual and interpretive approach to power dynamics based on a narrative approach (Elliott, 2005; Makkonen et al., 2012). Additionally, we considered the power and power asymmetry in the context of international business relationships.

Although research on business-to-business relationships early acknowledged shifts in power among sides of the relationship (Håkansson & Gadde, 1992; Johnsen & Ford, 2001), which can be equated with power dynamics (Cowan et al., 2015; Cox et al., 2004; Lacoste & Johnsen, 2015), relatively little research has been done to explain how such dynamics occur. Our book fills this gap some by presenting theoretical underpinnings and the results of longitudinal case study research of power dynamics in buyer-supplier relationships (subsection 2.2) and also research presented at other studies including studies on the power-related tactics of the weaker suppliers in relationship with dominant buyers (studies such us: Cowan et al., 2015; Lacoste & Johnsen, 2015; Pérez & Cambra-Fierro, 2015; Siemieniako & Mitręga, 2018a).

This book contributes to B2B strategy literature, which has largely ignored the longitudinal aspect of multifaceted power asymmetry in relationships between buying and selling companies (Hopkinson & Blois, 2014). The research provides evidence of power dynamics that were triggered by relationship development, those that were mainly initiated one-sidedly, as well as those that were contingent on changes within the larger supply chain relationship structure.

Specifically, the actions undertaken for strengthening one's own competencies in key areas of the supply chain increase the likelihood of better bargaining position in the existing business accounts and through expanding relationship portfolio. Our reasoning presented in the book corresponds well with conceptualising non-mediated power leveraging as a very positive device in managing business relationships (Benton & Maloni, 2005; Leonidou et al., 2019), however it also goes beyond these claims showing that in a long-run, non-mediated power can be a very useful and legitimate instrument in mitigating hegemony of customer-supplier relationships (Johnsen et al., 2020)

In each dyadic business relationship that we studied and presented in this book, but including also our previous research (e.g. Makkonen et al., 2021; Pfajfar et al., 2019; Siemieniako & Mitręga, 2018a; Zadykowicz et al., 2020) power dynamics was related to a specific set of asymmetry dynamics with regard to different sources of power that were specific and complex. This meant a particular side gaining an advantage in relation to some sources of power in combination with a weakness in relation to other sources of power. In sum, these unique combinations related to the level of power asymmetry cannot be treated as ultimate goals, but rather as certain states in the relationship that cause specific consequences and will be subject to further change – both intentional and unintentional under the influence of external factors outside the specific business relationship.

Importantly, longitudinal studies (e.g. Lacoste & Johnsen, 2015; Nyaga et al., 2013) illustrated that power dynamics may be sometimes extremely lengthy process and power asymmetry rather does not change with the same pace with regard to its all micro-elements. For example, case study research (see subsections 2.2) shows that buyer-supplier relationships may be clearly asymmetrical with regard to coercive power for two decades and such dominance may be later broken eventually, but only after shifts in other power sources (i.e. expert, informational). We call for implementing strategic approach towards using power in business relationships, i.e. anticipating consequences for relationship and for performance of such actions and applying long-term perspective.

The longitudinal case study research on power dynamics in buyer-supplier relationships presented in subsection 2.2, and the results of other research (Lacoste & Johnsen, 2015; Siemieniako & Mitręga, 2018a), allow to identify not only multi-dimensional character of power dynamics but also its multi-directional nature, which means that shifting power towards one side of a dyad may be continued by further power shift towards another side of a dyad.

Further we evidenced that these dynamics could be cyclical, and are driven by partners orientation at finding "relationship golden mean" and rejecting such relationship forms, which are treated as too risky. The research presented in subsection 2.2 provided also an evidence that "ideal" or "full" power symmetry is rather abstract in business relationships. On the other hand, this research provided the evidence that once such "appropriate" set of power asymmetries dimensions is found it stays in relationship for longer period. Using other words, the power (a)symmetry in business relationships is not that ephemeral, so it can be treated as manageable business factor.

Managerial implications

The reasoning presented in the book motivates managers involved in long-term relationships, firstly to carefully analyse their own and their partners' power positions with regard to mediated and non-mediated power, and, secondly, to evaluate how this power structure impacts on the value that is divided between business partners. Managers should analyse which levels of power asymmetry are the best for the relationship and how a variety of factors can influence power position shifts. We demonstrate the need to implement an interactive approach to power-related tactics by emphasising the perceptual and interpretivist nature of power dynamics in business relationships.

Like Siemieniako and Mitręga (2018b) concluded in their study, we believe that in general, the party being initially dominated should try to improve non-mediated power, which usually means developing competencies and delivering more relationship value to powerful partner. On the other hand the dominating party should support the weaker partner in that power shift, because it finally leverages economic- and non-economic relationship benefits. Power shifts with regard to mediated power sources are also possible, but should be facilitated very carefully, because they seem to be most acceptable, when they appear as somewhat "natural" consequence in evolution of non-mediated power. For example, the focal company may gain some "reward power" after building an image of an expert, because such power emerges, when business partner needs some further adjustments and cooperative actions. Additionally, the focal company should always try to build and keep good relationship atmosphere in business relationships, especially some close ties on interpersonal level. Specifically, it prevents the dominating side from using coercive power, which could easily hamper relationship development and result in relationship dissolution. Furthermore the results of our research (subsection 2.2) and the research of Siemieniako and Mitręga (2018a) demonstrated that substantial changes in multifaceted power asymmetry do not cause relationship dissolution and can even facilitate the relationship atmosphere without making the relationship problematic in terms of its economic value.

Managers of powerful companies should take into consideration that using a power advantage, e.g. by requesting a partner to make substantial investment in the relationship, may largely improve the partner's position with regard to non-mediated power, especially expert and referent power. In turn, these changes may likely interlink with partners' attempts to mitigate their initial disadvantage with regard to mediated power, e.g. by requesting major changes to contractual terms. In such situations, managers should carefully analyse the history of a given relationship, to retrospectively identify interaction patterns and anticipate further developments. For example, if "bluffing" was already noticed in a partner's behaviour, then some requests can logically be ignored. Additionally, managers should very much take into consideration not only a partner's behaviour within a relationship, but also the partner's changing power position in the context of the whole supply chain. Our research (subsection 2.2) shows that this is always a matter of interpretation in the wider context of the business that the partners are embedded in, as sometimes the stronger network position of a supply chain partner can be treated as the main factor that increases a partner's non-mediated power. It is visible especially in the power asymmetrical relationships of SME's and large corporations (e.g. Harness et al., 2018; Siemieniako & Mitręga, 2018a). It is the matter of referent power, which means dependence on own weaker partner's identification with stronger partner, rather than on intentional tactics of the powerful partner itself (Harness et al., 2018). Siemieniako and Mitręga (2018a) case study research revealed that a weaker supplier, after many years of such an embedded relationship with an MNC as a buyer, seeks both to maintain the benefits in working with this dominant partner and to become more independent by reducing the embeddedness in the relationship with that partner.

International marketing managers can use power to manage conflict and/ or increase performance in international distribution channels depending on the situation, context and time. Specifically, managers should use non-coercive power to decrease dysfunctional/emotional relationship conflict, and coercive power to decrease functional/cognitive/task conflict. This study draws a parallel between power and conflict resolution strategies, a link that remains underexplored in the extant literature. We propose that managers exercise non-coercive power in the case of applying "problem solving" or "compromise" conflict resolution styles, or when choosing a win-win strategy in international business negotiations. Similarly, managers should exercise coercive power when choosing "accommodation", "obligingness", "competition or aggression", "defiance" and "manipulation or dominance" means of handling conflicts, or when applying a win-lose strategy in international business negotiations. This has important implications for cross-cultural management. On the one hand, as the Japanese were found to negotiate following a 100% win-win strategy (Deresky, 2017), their international business partners should exercise solely non-coercive power, as the application of coercive power would lead to dissolution of such business relationships. On the other hand, the Spanish were found to negotiate according to a win-lose strategy in 70% of cases (Deresky, 2017), so international business partners should exercise coercive power, as the use of non-coercive power might significantly decrease their negotiation position with regard to Spanish partners in such relationships.

Research implications and limitations

In sections 1 and 2, although we have analysed and presented research based on quantitative studies (e.g. Harness et al., 2018; Nyaga et al., 2013), our main reasoning about power tactics and power dynamics is based on qualitative research, especially case studies (e.g. Cowan et al., 2015; Lacoste & Johnson, 2015). Consequently, the results of these studies we used are limited to a small group of buyer-supplier relationship types and therefore cannot be generalised uncritically. We propose to conduct further qualitative research, which can extend the findings of the works cited in this book to the context of different industries and different types of relationships. We call for more quantitative studies with regards to power dynamics in dyadic buyer-supplier asymmetrical relationships, e.g. dyadic survey on the large sample of buyer-supplier relationships.

Apart from the methodological approach, the research presented is also limited in terms of its scope, focusing mainly on dyadic buyer-supplier relationships, and the power asymmetry shifts for these relationships were explored. Most studies presented in the book have not looked beyond the internal context of the buyer-supplier relationship. An exception are the studies by Cheung et al. (2010) and Wang (2011).

This book provides an important contribution to the understanding of international business relationships by looking at them through the lens of headquarters-subsidiary relationships. Power distance seems to have a strong explanatory power for headquarters and subsidiaries' behaviour in their relationship (e.g. Drogendijk & Holm, 2012), thus we urge researchers to include power distance in their research on international business relationships, either as a direct antecedent to exercised power, or as a moderator of the relationship between exercised power and behavioural response. Scholars studying international knowledge transfer could benefit from the application of power in their research models. Finally, scholars could apply the concepts of weight and voice (Bouquet & Birkinshaw, 2008) in their future research on external business-to-business relationships, thereby clarifying the role of both business partners as possible sources of role conflict, and improving our understanding of the relationship atmosphere in the international business context.

References

Benton, W. C., & Maloni, M. (2005). The influence of power driven buyer/seller relationships on supply chain satisfaction. *Journal of Operations Management*, 23(1), 1–22.

Blomqvist, K., Hurmelina, P., & Seppanen, R. (2005). Playing the collaboration game right: Balancing trust and contracting, *Technovation*, 25(5), 497–505.

Bouquet, C., & Birkinshaw, J. (2008). Weight versus voice: How foreign subsidiaries gain attention from corporate headquarters. *Academy of Management Journal*, 51(3), 577–601.

Cheung, M. S., Myers, M. B., & Mentzer, J. T. (2010). Does relationship learning lead to relationship value? A cross-national supply chain investigation. *Journal of Operations Management*, 28(6), 472–487.

Cowan, K., Paswan, A. K., & Van Steenburg, E. (2015). When inter-firm relationship benefits mitigate power asymmetry. *Industrial Marketing Management*, 48, 140–148.

Cox, A., Watson, G., Lonsdale, C., & Sanderson, J. (2004). Managing appropriately in power regimes: Relationship and performance management in 12 supply chain cases. *Supply Chain Management: International Journal*, 9(5), 357–371.

Dahl, R. A. (1957). The concept of power. *Behavioral Science*, 2(3), 201–215.

Deresky, H. (2017). *International management: Managing across borders and cultures*. 9th ed. Harlow: Pearson.

Drogendijk, R., & Holm, U. (2015). Cultural distance or cultural positions? Analysing the effect of culture on the HQ – subsidiary relationship. In *Knowledge, networks and power* (pp. 366–392). London: Palgrave Macmillan.

Elliott, J. (2005). *Using narrative in social research: Qualitative and quantitative approaches*. London: Sage.

Emerson, R. M. (1962). Power-dependence relations. *American Sociological Review*, 31–41.

Håkansson, H., & Gadde, L.-E. (1992). Supplier relations. In *Professional purchasing* (pp. 59–77). Routledge: London.

Harness, D., Ranaweera, C., Karjaluoto, H., & Jayawardhena, C. (2018). The role of negative and positive forms of power in supporting CSR alignment and commitment between large firms and SMEs. *Industrial Marketing Management*, 75, 17–30.

Hopkinson, G. C., & Hingley, M. K. (2005). Power to all our friends? Living with imbalance in supplier–retailer relationships. *Industrial Marketing Management*, 34(8), 848–858.

Johnsen, R. E., & Ford, D. (2001). *Asymmetrical and symmetrical customer–supplier relationships: Contrasts, evolution and strategy*. Proceedings of the 17th IMP Conference, Oslo, Norway.

Johnsen, R. E., Lacoste, S., & Meehan, J. (2020). Hegemony in asymmetric customer-supplier relationships. *Industrial Marketing Management*, 87, 63–75.

Lacoste, S., & Johnsen, E. (2015). Supplier–customer relationships: A case study of power dynamics. *Journal of Purchasing and Supply Management*, 21, 229–240.

Leonidou, L. C., Aykol, B., Spyropoulou, S., & Christodoulides, P. (2019). The power roots and drivers of infidelity in international business relationships. *Industrial Marketing Management*, 78, 198–212.

Makkonen, H., Aarikka-Stenroos, L., & Olkkonen, R. (2012). Narrative approach in business network process research: Implications for theory and methodology. *Industrial Marketing Management*, 41(2), 287–299.

Makkonen, H., Siemieniako, D., & Mitręga, M. (2021). Structural and behavioural power dynamics in buyer-supplier relationships: A perceptions-based framework and a research agenda. *Technology Analysis & Strategic Management*, 1–15.

Nyaga, G. N., Lynch, D. F., Marshall, D., & Ambrose, E. (2013). Power asymmetry, adaptation and collaboration in dyadic relationships involving a powerful partner. *Journal of Supply Chain Management*, 49(3), 42–65.

Oukes, T., von Raesfeld, A., & Groen, A. (2019). Power in a startup's relationships with its established partners: Interactions between structural and behavioural power. *Industrial Marketing Management*, 80, 68–83.

Pérez, L., & Cambra-Fierro, J. (2015). Learning to work in asymmetric relationships: Insights from the computer software industry. *Supply Chain Management: An International Journal*.

Pfajfar, G., Shoham, A., Brenčič, M. M., Koufopoulos, D., Katsikeas, C. S., & Mitręga, M. (2019). Power source drivers and performance outcomes of functional and dysfunctional conflict in exporter–importer relationships. *Industrial Marketing Management*, 78, 213–226.

Siemieniako, D., & Mitręga, M. (2018a). Improving power position with regard to non-mediated power sources–the supplier's perspective. *Industrial Marketing Management*, 70, 90–100.

Siemieniako, D., & Mitręga, M. (2018b). *Is it good to balance power in a buyer-seller "business marriage" and how it happens?* 34th IMP Conference: From Business to Research and Back Again, Kedge Business School, Marseille Campus, Marseille, France 4–7.09.2018. Available at: www.impgroup.org/paper_view.php?viewPaper=9889 [data of access: 2021.11.12].

Wang, C. H. (2011). The moderating role of power asymmetry on the relationships between alliance and innovative performance in the high-tech industry. *Technological Forecasting and Social Change*, 78(7), 1268–1279.

Wolfe, R. J., & McGinn, K. L. (2005). Perceived relative power and its influence on negotiations. *Group Decision and Negotiation*, 14(1), 3–20.

Zadykowicz, A., Chmielewski, K., & Siemieniako, D. (2020). Proactive customer orientation and joint learning capabilities in collaborative machine to machine innovation technology development: The case study of automotive equipment manufacturer. *Oeconomia Copernicana*, 11(3), 415–423.

Index

Note: Page numbers in *italics* indicate figures and page numbers in **bold** indicate tables.